EVER SINCE ADAM AND EVE

EVER SINCE ADAM AND EVE

by Terry Hekker

WILLIAM MORROW AND COMPANY, INC.

NEW YORK   1979

Grateful acknowledgment is made for permission to use the following previously published material:

Eight lines from "What Every Woman Knows" by Phyllis McGinley, from *Times Three* by Phyllis McGinley. Copyright © 1960 by Phyllis McGinley. All rights reserved. Reprinted by permission of Viking Penguin, Inc.

Portions of Chapter 16 from "There's No Place Like Home" by Terry Martin Hekker, reprinted with permission from TV GUIDE® Magazine. Copyright © 1976 by Triangle Publications, Inc., Radnor, Pennsylvania.

"Satisfactions of Housewifery" by Terry Hekker, December 20, 1977, Op-Ed. © 1977 by The New York Times Company. Reprinted by permission.

Library of Congress Cataloging in Publication Data

Hekker, Terry.
    Ever since Adam and Eve.

    1. Housewives—United States.   2. Mothers—United States.
I. Title.
HQ759.H445   301.42'7   79-363
ISBN 0-688-03442-X

BOOK DESIGN   CARL WEISS

First Edition

1   2   3   4   5   6   7   8   9   10

To the ladies

Marie O'Donohue Martin (1914–1965)

and

Susan Larkin O'Donohue (1880–1963)

They are what this book is all about.*

---

* I considered dedicating this to my husband until I noticed how many women dedicated first books to their supportive and understanding husbands and the husbands subsequently decided to support and understand a younger woman. Why tempt the fates?

INTRODUCTION

WARNING: HANDLE WITH CARE (OR THE STORE won't take it back). You see, this book is not what is known in the trade as a "hot item." For your sake, I hope you got it from the library or borrowed it from a friend. If you laid out good money, perhaps you could return it. If you haven't scribbled in it or torn the jacket, you might be able to exchange it for a book by a *real* author.

That's the thing. I'm not. An author that is. I'm also not an expert, an authority, a celebrity, or someone who's had sex with one. I'm not even a convicted felon, more's the pity. And if the author sounds dull, the subject is worse.

What you, probably inadvertently, have just begun reading is a book about the world's second oldest but most obsolete profession—housewifery. Attempts to salt it with sex and violence have proved fruitless and four-letter words looked hopelessly out of place.

Consideration was given to lacing the book with charts and surveys and statistics to make it relevant, and as much as I've always yearned to be relevant I just can't bring myself to have faith in all those num-

bers. When one of my brothers was studying account-
ing, a worldly-wise professor told him, "Figures don't
lie but liars figure." Numbers lend themselves to inter-
pretation and I have lately seen the same figures used
to justify why the American family has never been
stronger and to prove that the American family is on
its way down the tube. Besides, everyone knows that
if you have two similar keys in your pocket there
should be a fifty-fifty chance of pulling out the right
one first, and 90 percent of the time you don't. Statistics
are less reliable than oil-tanker captains.

Omission of statistics is admittedly more of a handicap to the success of this book than even the lack of
sex and violence. For we are a society obsessed with
surveys. There was one recently that determined on
an island off California 14 percent of the female
sea gulls were lesbians (and we know that kind of
thing would never go among Nantucket sea gulls). I
read of a clinical evaluation of group sex that proved
the people who engage in it usually have beige
drapes. (Is it, perhaps, some kind of signal?) An ex-
haustive survey of the differences between conservatives and liberals pointed out that conservatives place
their houseplants on tables while liberals put theirs on
the floor. (Should not some attempt have been made
to ascertain why conservatives have more tables?) Can
you imagine the loss if you died never knowing these
things? Particularly if you died of cancer or heart disease or any one of the illnesses for which there is not
enough research money.

Common sense isn't so common, as my grandmother
used to say. Today everything has to be proved. A

couple of years ago a very thorough and scientific study was carried out, paid for by HEW, to determine why small children have injuries from riding tricycles. Thousands of dollars later, researchers arrived at the answer: Because they fall off. Grandma wouldn't have paid a nickel for that news.

Besides not having statistics, this book is also bereft of expert opinions. There was temptation to at least interview some family experts, but they're all writing their own books. Books on how to be a "modern parent," "single parent," "homosexual parent," "adoptive parent" or even "nonparent." They are doing volumes of advice on "coping with the underachiever," "coping with the overachiever," "hints for mothers who breast-feed" and "help for mothers who think that's yucky."

And while all of these experts have their points, the answers to many of life's dilemmas are often as obvious as a sunrise. I read those books about being my own pal and looking out for *numero uno* and I'm terrific but you're so-so; and it took almost a thousand pages for those authorities to say what my grandmother expressed with one old Irish saying: "Please yourself and you'll know you pleased somebody."

There was some thought in publishing circles that a book excluding statistics and expert opinions but purporting to concern endangered species should be written by an anthropologist. I insisted however that if Jane Goodall could know so much about gorillas from observing them for years, I should be able to write about housewives after being one for years. Also my mother was one, as was her mother. I am, in fact, probably the zillionth in an unbroken succession of housewives. And I am probably the last.

Regardless of approaching obsolescence, as a practicing housewife I have grown weary of being examined and interpreted by outsiders. All kinds of experts pontificate about the American housewife—her problems, her oppression, her pitiful values, her ring-around-the-collar, stuffing-instead-of-potatoes mentality. But seldom does an actual housewife get a chance to give her version. We are told how we should feel, what we should want, but our needs, emotions and goals are neither considered nor appreciated.

My knowledge of this subject was picked up "in the field," as they say in academic circles. It comes from being the oldest of six children and the oldest of thirty-three grandchildren. Not, please note, the oddest— there's some hefty competition on that score. I have been married for twenty-three years to a man toward whom I have a cheap physical attraction. And I have five children, aged nine to twenty-two, one of them a female girl. I am, in short, a wife, a mother, a homemaker. And I wouldn't have it any other way.

I am not, as you have been suspecting, a writer. Two years ago *TV Guide* published a story I wrote about having television commercials filmed in my house, but that was the extent of my literary career. In December 1977, because of my frustrations with, and amusement at, the reactions to my profession, I sent an account of my observations to *The New York Times*. They printed it on their Op Ed page and then newspapers all over the country and around the world reprinted it. *Good Housekeeping* ran it in their May 1978 issue and mail poured in from fellow housewives, and ex-housewives and career women. Many wrote lengthy and articulate letters about their positions, and problems surfaced that I had not even considered. Out of those letters and my own experiences came this book.

My experiences are just that—what I've witnessed in my own life and the lives of those around me. As a small child in Brooklyn I watched my grandmother cope with her family and, as her oldest child, I saw how Mama dealt with hers. So no questionnaires were sent out and no charts drawn up, no psychological insights sought and no anthropological conclusions drawn.

There is nothing in these pages that I didn't know before I wrote the *Times* column, but I would have felt it presumptuous to undertake a book until the overwhelming response to the column proved my own observations and feelings to be almost universal.

The idea that anyone will pay money for my words quite staggers me. Especially since I have been known to inflict unsolicited opinions on startled strangers in dentists' waiting rooms and check-out lines at the Super-Duper (a practice that mortifies my children). My conscience bothers me to the extent that I insisted this book have a red binding (because I recall an aunt who asked the Book-of-the-Month Club to send her any books with red covers since she just wanted them for effect anyway). Beyond its decorative value—since it's not heavy enough for a doorstop or thick enough to boost the baby up to the table—all you have are the uncorroborated observations of a housewife circa 1979.

CHAPTER

1

T*he New York Times*, Op-Ed page, December 20, 1977

SOUTH NYACK, N.Y.—My son lied about it on his college application. My husband mutters it under his breath when asked. And I had grown reluctant to mention it myself.

The problem is my occupation. But the statistics on women that have come out since the Houston conference have given me a new outlook. I have ceased thinking of myself as obsolete and begun to see myself as I really am—an endangered species. Like the whooping crane and snow leopard, I deserve attentive nurturing and perhaps a distinctive metal tag on my foot. Because I'm one of the last of the dying breed of human females designated, Occupation: Housewife.

I know it's nothing to crow about. I realize that when people discuss their professions at parties I am more of a pariah than a hooker or a loan shark. I have been castigated, humiliated and scorned. In an age of do your own thing, it's clear no one meant me. I've been told (patiently and a little louder than necessary, as one does with a small child) that I am an anachronism

17

(except that they avoid such a big word). I have been made to feel so outmoded that I wouldn't be surprised to discover that, like a carton of yogurt, I have an expiration date stamped on my bottom.

I once treasured a small hope that history might vindicate me. After all, nursing was once just such a shameful occupation, suitable for only the lowest of women. But I abandoned any thought that my occupation would ever become fashionable again, just as I had to stop counting on full-figured women coming back into style. I'm a hundred years too late on both counts.

Now, however, thanks to all these new statistics, I see a brighter future for myself. Today, fewer than 16 percent of American families have a full-time housewife-mother. Comparing that with previous figures, at the rate it's going I calculate I am less than eight years away from being the last housewife in the country. And then I intend to be impossible.

I shall demand enormous fees to go on talk shows, and charge for my autograph. Anthropologists will study my feeding and nesting habits through field glasses and keep notebooks detailing my every move. That is, if no one gets the bright idea that I'm so unique that I must be put behind sealed glass like the Book of Kells. In any event, I can expect to be a celebrity and to be pampered. I cannot, though, expect to get even.

There's no getting even for years of being regarded as stupid or lazy, or both. For years of being considered unproductive (unless you count five children, which no one does). For years of being viewed as a parasite, living off a man (except by my husband whose opinion doesn't seem to matter). For years of fetching other women's children after they'd thrown up in the lunchroom, because I have nothing better to do, or probably there is nothing I do better, while their mothers have "careers." For years of caring for five children and a big house and constantly being asked when I'm going to work.

I come from a long line of women, most of them more Edith Bunker than Betty Friedan, who never knew they were unfulfilled. I can't testify that they were happy, but they were cheerful. And if they lacked "meaningful relationships," they cherished relations who meant something. They took pride in a clean, comfortable home and satisfaction in serving a good meal because no one had explained to them that the only work worth doing is that for which you get paid.

They enjoyed raising their children because no one ever told them that little children belonged in church basements and their mothers belonged somewhere else. They lived, very frugally, on their husbands' paychecks because they didn't realize that it's more important to have a bigger house and a second car than it is to rear your own children. And they were so incredibly ignorant that they died never suspecting they'd been failures.

That won't hold true for me. I don't yet perceive myself as a failure, but it's not for want of being told I am.

The other day, years of condescension prompted me to fib in order to test a theory. At a party where most of the guests were business associates of my husband, a Ms. Put-down asked me who I was. I told her I was

Jack Hekker's wife. That had a galvanizing effect on her. She took my hand and asked if that was all I thought of myself—just someone's wife? I wasn't going to let her in on the five children, but when she persisted I mentioned them but told her that they weren't mine, that they belonged to my dead sister. And then I basked in the glow of her warm approval.

It's an absolute truth that whereas you are considered ignorant to stay home to raise your children, it is quite heroic to do so for someone else's children. Being a housekeeper is acceptable (even to the Social Security office) as long as it's not *your* house you're keeping. And treating a husband with attentive devotion is altogether correct as long as he's not *your* husband.

Sometimes I feel like Alice in Wonderland. But lately, mostly, I feel like an endangered species.

The reaction to that column was overwhelming. I would prefer to think it was triggered by my literary genius, but that was clearly not the case. What prompted the response was the identification of a problem, a prejudice, which hundreds of women felt they'd been facing alone. Beautiful letters came from elderly women saying how nice it was to see their philosophy expressed by a young woman. (How nice, at forty-five, to be thought of as a young woman!) Poignant letters were sent by widowers who'd discovered their housewives had been irreplaceable treasures.

Surprisingly, more than half of the letters came from working women and these fell into four clear categories. The first group said they were glad they'd stayed at home until their children were off to school.

The next group said they regretted not staying home those first few precious years. The third group was resentful and often bitter, claiming they'd been pushed out to work by husbands wanting better cars and bigger homes.

The fourth group was most intriguing. These letters came from career women, mostly childless, often single, and written on stationery whose letterheads indicated they had achieved considerable success. Their gripe was with the "put-down" attitude of "women's libbers" in the business world who they felt had divided women and antagonized men. They were articulate and persuasive, but this aspect of the women's movement is something I am not remotely qualified to comment on. In the immortal words of Pierre Salinger, "I may be plucky but I'm not stupid."

Out of hundreds of letters, only ten attacked my position or more precisely what they assumed was my position. All of the clichés about housewives surfaced in these letters which, ironically, started out saying that there's no prejudice against housewives. One psychologist stated that we are not stereotyped and ended by saying that I was obviously a fraud anyway, since no housewife could write well enough to make the *Times*. Hookers and ladies' maids write books, but a writing housewife is somehow akin to a singing dog.

Attempts were made by two well-meaning feminists to liberate me. I was informed that I was being exploited by my children, a phrase that gave them a good chuckle. The truth is, my offspring are threatening to sell the "real, untold story" of my motherhood to the *National Enquirer*. They claim to have hard evidence that only McDonald's has stood between them and malnutrition. And that my cavalier attitude toward the laundry has caused them to spend their formative years in damp socks.

I was called a traitor to my sisters, a white Aunt Jemima, and therapy was suggested—everything from *est* to encounter. One mentioned that my occupation was a symbol of oppression and that I was no more than a "happy slave" (now came my husband's turn to chuckle). A man wrote that I obviously disregarded the role of the strong father in raising children. Chuckles all around because our children contend that Uganda is run more democratically than our house.

The opposition I expected, and would have considered valid, never surfaced. No one mentioned the elitist element involved since poor women haven't the opportunity to choose between work and homemaking. And only my fellow housewives mentioned the great good luck it takes to find a husband willing and able to support a family.

I was appalled, but not surprised, to find that because I am a housewife I was prejudged to be anti-feminist, anti-liberation and reactionary. It's somewhat like telling a black tap dancer that he's obviously anti-civil rights. The crime is called "reinforcing negative images," and it's a bum rap.

I cannot imagine that there is a woman alive today who is opposed to equality for all women. We want it for ourselves and we demand it for our daughters. Unfortunately, while united by our doubts we are divided by our convictions. At the risk of seeming hopelessly old-fashioned, I believe most of our problems could be mitigated by harking back to the Golden Rule, by wanting no more and no less freedom of choice and dignity for all women than we want for ourselves.

The thing is, girls, we are one terrific sex. We are flexible and adjustable, understanding and compassionate. We may be prone to chatter but we're good listeners. Women generally make fine doctors because they actually hear your symptoms. We are strong and able to adapt. We are survivors.

We have a long history of supporting, encouraging and helping each other. While men were out jousting on the fields and competing in the marketplace, women were helping each other give birth and meet death, lending a hand or a cup of sugar. We are capable of close friendships while few men find it easy to sustain warm relationships with other men.

But now as we reach out for the full equality that is long overdue, why are we allowing ourselves to be fragmented by labels? Housewives, career girls, feminists, libbers, whatever—aren't we all, like Kipling's Colonel's Lady and Rosie O'Grady, sisters under the skin?

And why be so quick to take offense at being referred to as "girls"? My dear husband ran for public office last year and got into more trouble for referring to "women" as "girls" than he did for referring to "sanitary landfill" as "garbage."

CHAPTER

FROM THE TIME I WAS A FRONT-TOOTHLESS LITTLE girl in a white communion dress it was made clear that boys came first. They got to walk up the aisle before the girls and could be altar boys. They could grow up and become priests and say mass on the altar and we could grow up and become nuns and clean the altar.

We all came to realize that women have not had equality under the law and have, historically, been second-class citizens. Pagan civilizations treated women as chattel or toys. Aristotle wrote that a female is a female by virtue of a certain lack of qualities and is afflicted with a natural defectiveness. Plato thanked God first that he was created free and not a slave and second that he'd been created a man and not a woman. Roman law limited the rights of women because of their imbecility and the instability of their sex.

Christianity wasn't much kinder. Saint Augustine claimed woman is a creature neither decisive nor constant. And Saint Thomas proclaimed woman an incidental being, an imperfect man. Small wonder then that discrimination against women, which was so unfair in

27

business and government, extended into organized religion (where ironically women have traditionally provided the supporting backbone). It is now possible for a woman to serve as leader of a major world power, but she can't be a priest and faces enormous odds to be a minister or rabbi.

A priest who wrote to me presuming he'd found an ally in his fight against the E.R.A. said the nuns in his parish were behind it, unaware that it was the work of the Devil. He is undoubtedly a fine man and meant well, but his letter disturbed me because it reinforced the very image of the housewife that I most profoundly resent. He was congratulating me for being one woman who knew her place and had accepted her secondary role with holy resignation. He was barking up the wrong housewife.

A professional woman at a dinner party said, "My husband adored your column. He'd *love* to have me under his thumb like that." (My husband almost choked on his ice cream.) Occupation: housewife obviously conjures up visions of soft-spoken subservient women licking their husbands' hands. Compared to housewives, psoriasis has a positive image.

Almost every letter sent by a fellow housewife mentioned being treated as an inferior by most working women and some men as well. Housewives from California, Texas, Saudi Arabia and Iowa told similar stories of being regarded as nitwits or being solicitously urged to "take some courses in consciousness raising and assertiveness." Mostly by people who could have benefited from some courses in manners and sensitivity training.

The most touching letters came from elderly women who felt the women's movement, with its emphasis on fulfillment through paid jobs, had robbed them of their last remaining treasure—the pride they'd had in raising their families. They were resentful of a younger generation that regarded their life's work as meaningless.

The leaders of the movement vociferously deny being anti-housewife, but they must admit to appearing that way. And although I've heard my former neighbor Ms. Friedan deny such a position, in her book *The Feminine Mystique*, she proclaimed that housework is suitable employment for feeble-minded girls and can be done by an eight-year-old. Now I don't know much about feeble-minded girls, but I've had an eight-year-old and I wonder how much Ms. Friedan would pay him to clean her place.

Housework is just like every other profession, because the truth is that anyone can do any job. Doing it *right* is the trick. I could sing arias at the Met or perform appendectomies if I didn't mind being hit with rotten tomatoes or a lawsuit. But if you go with the old adage that anything worth doing is worth doing well, then your work, whether it be street cleaning or sitting on the Supreme Court, becomes more challenging and meaningful. We bemoan the fact that few people today seem to take pride in their work, while we simultaneously equate dollar values with the respect we accord our fellow men and women. Housework is a low-paying (or nonpaying) job. Ergo it is worthless and those who choose to do it are dismissed as inferiors.

All right, you say, so housewives are looked down

upon. They're unfashionable like saddle shoes. So what? Well, first, it is an injustice to categorize the members of any profession: all doctors are money-hungry, lawyers are thieves, policemen are on-the-take, actresses have loose morals, housewives are stupid and lazy.

Second, our self-image is often a reflection of the way others perceive us and in that respect today's housewife is the classic victim. We have been subjected to discrimination of the most insidious kind because it is so generously mixed with condescension. Hundreds of letters from fellow housewives reaffirm my experiences as universal.

But now comes the double whammy, and this is where the discrimination becomes most cruel. The devoted and efficient homemaker-mother has seen her children grow more self-sufficient, her home more organized, and she wants (and often desperately needs) gainful employment. Not only does her own battered self-esteem create problems, but a prospective employer is likely to disregard her because of his low opinion of housewives. A woman who hasn't "worked" in ten or fifteen or twenty years must be lazy and unreliable. Maybe she drinks. "What can someone with such demonstrably poor motivation offer my business?"

The truth is that most housewives have remained at home because they are conscientious about their responsibilities and will be just as dependable as employees. Since housework rarely involves deadlines or critical supervision (except by the occasional mother-in-law), housewives more than anyone else need to be self-starting and self-motivated. Going out into the business world they are more mature and reliable than girls fresh out of school. "Former occupation: house-wife" should be an inducement, not a handicap.

So much mail came from this group of women, many back in school learning marketable skills. One mid-western housewife wrote, "I've returned to college in a woman's reentry program with women of all ages. Many feel inadequate because of the put-down of housewives. Your article made me feel so much better about myself that I had copies made to hand out in class." I hesitated to quote that letter, it seemed so self-serving. But it indicates a real problem and an attitude that deserves to be changed.

Letters came from former housewives who were often astonished to find out that they're just as well informed and intelligent as their career-girl contemporaries, whose job-for-pay is often less stimulating and rewarding than housework.

Why then are housewives held in such poor regard? Why does housework have such a bad name? It is judged to be repetitious and boring, but so is brain surgery or starring in a Broadway show, driving a bus or modeling Parisian fashions.

Whoever said that housework stifles creativity never had to make three pounds of chopped chuck and two chickens feed seven people for a week. They never had to furnish a fifteen-by-twenty living room with $180, and they never had to fill out a college application for a kid who played one sport and didn't join any clubs and had to be made to sound like the all-around great student. Isaac Asimov never wrote fiction like I've written on college applications.

Neither H. nor R. Block ever juggled figures like

the average housewife, meeting $500 worth of bills with $375, and Claes Oldenburg may be a genius with soft sculpture, but did he ever cover a ten-foot couch with a three-yard remnant? Could Picasso have pulled a rocker off the curb on junk day and made it a more handsome addition to that empty living room? Could Henry Kissinger be diplomatic enough to convince each child that he got the best room, the niftiest first name and is the family favorite? Could Julia Child make a tastier peanut butter-and-jelly sandwich? Could Dr. Spock be more comforting to the flu victim? Could Mario Andretti deliver four kids to four different locations in a twenty-mile radius in fifteen minutes? Only air-traffic controllers can compete with the challenges most housewives face routinely.

Besides being called boring and repetitious, housework is also maligned for robbing you of adult conversation. Let me tell you, adult conversation is more overrated than southern cooking. When I worked my boss talked incessantly about two subjects: the deplorable state of the Long Island Rail Road and the equally distressing condition of his digestive tract. My youngest child is Noel Coward by comparison.

And from what I remember, my coworkers weren't much for sparkling repartee either. The younger ones bragged about their romances and the older ones about their infirmities. I recall most of them as having been separated from tumors as big as grapefruit or cantaloupe. Children talk to you about how it must feel to be a bird or why you water plants when they haven't got mouths. They make up their own wonderful words. One of ours kept his hands warm with "knittens" and another followed a "bumpy" rabbit across the lawn. Children are direct and literal. Our third son was about four when, told he had his shoes on the wrong feet, he said, "But those are the only feet I got."

Teen-agers tell you about school and friends and failures and triumphs. One of our sons had a speech class where each student had to pick a controversial subject and discuss the pros and cons. He complained that one kid in the class was so dense, his subject was rape. (How do you argue pro-rape?) He then told about a girl who argued for premarital sex and discussed contraception, but she left out what he considered her most effective contraceptive—her face. His brother chimed in that the girl was so hot on premarital sex because it's the only kind she'll ever get.

One of our sons had to dress as a woman for a school play, and he complained bitterly about how tight my panty hose were. His brother finally told him, "Then whatever you do, don't pass gas. You'll blow your shoes off." And when one of the boys was attempting to take a photograph of an eclipse for his science class, his older brother told him, "You're too far away. Stand on a chair." So it's not Neil Simon. It still tops most of what I heard around the office.

I will admit there is the repetitious angle to housework. The Greek gods, who condemned Sisyphus to roll uphill a stone which always rolled back, really knew how to hurt a guy. But Sisyphus had it no worse than any housewife. Endless loads of dirty laundry, doomed to return to the hamper within hours of being washed, dried and folded, can get you down.

Once, on vacation, we passed a nightclub featuring

nude men, and my husband asked me if that's something I'd like to see. I said no, but didn't realize until I thought about it later that my entire connotation with naked men is not erotic. I see nude men and I think "laundry." Because for every streaker in our house there's a pile of it waiting for me. The boys race down the hall yelling "Don't look," and I relentlessly shout back my grandmother's line, "I'd rather see a ghost."

C H A P T E R

3

WHEN I FIRST USED THE TERM "ENDANGERED species," it was to make a point satirically. But it is actually a very valid term, for full-time housewives are now all but extinct. A woman today can expect to live over seventy years and if she marries and plans to bear children, she likely has two in mind. If she has them in her mid-twenties, by her mid-thirties they will be in school most of the day and she'll want and need something else to do. Otherwise she can end up needing her children more than they need her.

In my grandmother's day the children didn't leave home until they married. Not one of her chicks established his own nest as a single person. Consequently, when the last one left home, Grandma was seventy-one and had only one leg to boot (or even to shoe). Hardly a hot item for the job market, although as a handicapped female senior citizen she might have seemed a treasure to a harried personnel officer trying to meet his quotas.

Very few grown children today live in their parents' home. A child who goes off to college at eighteen seldom returns for longer than it takes to eat everything in the refrigerator. And what woman will want to spend the last thirty years of her life rearranging the dust in an empty house? She won't even want the house. Taxes, utility bills and the scarcity of domestic help have conspired to make a house a luxury and a burden. As much as I love our rambling old Victorian home, the fact is that ours is probably the last big family to run through its halls. When it becomes too cumbersome for us it will be sold for a multiple dwelling, as most of the surrounding houses have been.

It's a marvelous old relic with a place for everything and everyone. It was, however, designed to be run by a "staff" and not by one disorganized Irish housekeeper (me). It has a butler's pantry but no butler and two maids' rooms complete with bells but no maids come a-running. Caring for it and its occupants has been two full-time jobs, but our days are numbered. Three of the children are already away in college and soon I must come to grips with the middle-age triple threat: menopause, the empty-nest syndrome and "What do I want to be when my children grow up?"

Grandma had it easier. All she really had to cope with were the hot flashes which, when you'd had your seventh child at forty-four, were more welcome than the flowers in spring. Her nest didn't empty, and why would she ever want to get a job when her husband already had one? She had no desire to find herself because she always knew who she was, where she belonged.

Her granddaughters have a harder time of it. We are unsure and confused. Her life ran down a rocky road, but ours is a proverbial steeplechase with one hurdle after another. When our children no longer consume all our energies, we are expected to start a career, to achieve and succeed on yet another level. We are expected not only to bear and nurture children, but to help support them as well. And through it all we are expected to look terrific, to avoid flabbiness, cellulite, wrinkles and gray hair. We have become jugglers with five balls in the air at once—husband, children, home, job and self-improvement. And do it all cheerfully, girls, cheerfully!

My grandmother, and yours too most probably, was expected to stay home and grow old gracefully. She not only didn't have to get a job, but she also didn't have to hold up her end of a mixed-doubles game or keep her girlish figure forever. Grandma had a tough life and, having barely survived a famine, calories were not an issue with her. And when you wash laundry by hand, lug it to the line and iron with a six-pound iron, you're not looking to spend your evenings at Elaine Powers.

In her day women were too busy and too frugal to spend time and money on themselves. I doubt that Grandma ever saw the inside of a beauty parlor. And because they didn't have opportunities to remodel, women accepted themselves and each other as God made them. I know women who've had so many nips and tucks their own mothers wouldn't recognize them. A cousin who's had two nose jobs no longer goes "Ah-choo" when she sneezes, but honks like a Canadian goose.

I only had one grandaunt who even wore falsies and

I can't forget that because she was so frugal that when she cut off their exaggerated nipples, she insisted on using them for corn pads.

So much is expected of today's women in terms of appearance. Okay, we get helpful suggestions from magazines. But I've followed them all with no visible improvement. I read where plucking your eyebrows into a thin line and applying proper eye makeup can give the "startled look of a young fawn." I followed the directions carefully and wound up with the startled look of a middle-aged woman who's just swallowed her gum. Grandma never even owned any makeup, and when her daughters convinced her she needed eyebrows (hers being so light as to be invisible), she took to drawing them on with the burnt ends of matchsticks.

Last week I saw a woman in the supermarket who I know is a grandmother, and she was wearing jeans tucked into cowboy boots and more Indian jewelry than a medicine man. Gone are the days when a grandmother could look like one. If Whistler painted his mother today she'd probably be portrayed running the Boston Marathon in a double-knit jogging suit. My grandmother (and Mama too) never even owned slacks. Grandma wore cotton housedresses, with a sweater added for winter. She had a black dress and a flowered silk dress and one coat which for special occasions was dressed up with those furs where each fox bites the tail of the one in front. She had a straw hat with flowers and a black hat with a dead bird on top. In those days Mrs. Astor was expected to look stylish, but firemen's wives were content to look neat:

a clean outfit, a scrubbed face and hair in a bun.

Not so today, and it is nifty that even women on limited budgets can manage to appear attractive and stylish. But it takes so much effort and gets to be a drag sometimes. The only thing I ever saw in favor of being a nun was I'd never have to set my hair again. Last year I got that frizzed hairdo to make me look "now" (I looked like I'd just now stuck a fork in the toaster). The Russian peasant outfit, I must admit, did make me look the part. All I needed to complete the effect was an old broom. And this spring when I went to buy a dress to wear to a retirement dinner, I had to choose between looking like an urban guerrilla or Little Bo-Peep.

If there is one word that covers the differences between our grandmothers' lives and our own, it is "choices." They had so few and we have so many, even in how we look and dress. But more importantly, in how we will live our lives.

When I was born, less than fifty years ago, the first grandchild in two large families, not one person looked down on me in my white wicker bassinet and said, "Someday she might be President," or "The way she blabbers all day she'll make a great lawyer." The highest hope held out for my future was that I'd make a good marriage. The way I was raised made it inevitable that I never seriously thought about any other life-style. Being a wife and mother was all I ever considered. And I was most fortunate to find a man who made it all right and good for me.

Many of my contemporaries weren't so lucky. It was the life they got, the one they'd been assured was best for them, but it was not what they really wanted. Unfortunately, most young women coming of age in the mid-1950s (as in all the preceding centuries) believed that marriage and homemaking were supposed to be the only goals they should have. Just the unloved and unclaimed girls went, reluctantly, into the job market. Or so we were told.

Whatever work we trained for in high school or college was not to prepare for a career, but for a skill we'd have "just in case" (something happened to our husbands). Teaching was a biggie. Nursing was another and secretarial skills were high on the list. And never thought of as the first steps in a growing career, but as viable alternatives just in case we picked a lemon in the garden of love.

Young women today have choices that I never considered and options my grandmother never dreamed of. But choices can prove a mixed blessing when immature and inexperienced girls are routinely forced to make difficult decisions and judgments. With so many avenues open to them, they have to pick not the easiest but the least perilous.

The absence of alternatives in the lives of most young women years ago was terribly wrong, but it sure made things simple. You knew just what was expected of you, all the boundaries were well marked, and if you were racked by indecision, it was over what dress to wear to a prom. Today's young women have tougher choices to make.

For instance, when I finished college and needed a roommate to share an apartment, the requirements were that she be about my dress size and cute enough to attract boys (since I was always, alas, the type who relied heavily on "personality"). Now, my friends' daughters must find a roommate of the same sexual persuasion, then determine if she'll bring home sleep-over dates, and if so are they likely to do unspeakable things that will frighten the cat?

When I was ready to marry, marriage contracts were unheard of; so was open marriage and trial marriage. If you had a yen for a guy the choices were holy wed-lock or living in sin—and the latter was guaranteed to send you to hell, ruin your reputation and kill your mother. Some choice! It may not have been right, but it sure made things simpler.

Marriage was, until very recently, an implied con-tract. He supports her while she manages his home and cares for his children. There was no need for deep dis-cussion of role reversal, conflicting careers or shared housework. Both partners knew just what was ex-pected of them and usually did it. Oh, occasionally he'd get up with the baby or she'd make pin money as an Avon lady, but for the most part each one pulled his or her preordained share of the load.

Historically, this arrangement had proved workable, and we women who married in the fifties envisioned a life very much like our mothers had before us. But then everything changed. Cropping up in quick succes-sion were women's liberation, consciousness raising, population explosion and the pill. Having spent our lives being told to be good daughters, good wives, good mothers, all of a sudden we were told, "Do your own thing." "Find yourself." Bearing many children stopped being noble and quickly became selfish. Being finan-

cially supported by a man ceased to be honorable and
for the very first time married women with jobs became
the rule instead of the exception. But most importantly,
the long-overdue equality of women started to become
a reality.

We came a long way, baby. And we owe thanks to
Margaret Sanger, who made birth control respectable,
and Dr. Rock, who gave us the pill. Because no
great change would have been possible for women as
long as having sex meant having babies. The leaders
of the women's movement would have you believe that
they gave birth to the liberated woman, when they
were never more than Johnny-come-lately midwives.
Women are not streaming into the marketplace merely
because some feminist or her book led the way. Women
are out working because they're not spending their
lives in obstetricians' waiting rooms. For the first time
in the history of our planet, girl babies are being born
whose anatomy is not their destiny.

Doors are swinging wide and women are going
through them into law school and medical school. They
don't know from just-in-case jobs. They may be starting as secretaries, but have their eyes on chairwoman
of the board. And those who choose to marry and have
babies know the time will come when they'll want an
outside job. It is no longer a question of whether you'll
go out to work, but when.

Even that was never true until now. Grandma never
dreamed of a job once she married and neither did
my mother. In fact, Mama spent a full, if short, life
without ever having a real job, except for one brief
stint in the yard goods department at B. Altman's right

before she got married. I heard about that because Dad loved to tell the story of picking her up at work one night and taking her to a fancy French restaurant to meet his boss. He said he'd never forget how young and lovely she looked, but when the waiter helped her off with her coat, Altman's scissors were still dangling around her neck.

CHAPTER

UNLIKE MANY ENDANGERED SPECIES, THE HOUSEWIFE is not becoming extinct because of heartless hunters or built-in obsolescence. Neither is she the victim of evolution but rather of revolution. For evolution requires small modifications through many generations while the housewife is endangered because of a revolution that took place in the course of one generation. It was my dubious luck to have the first cannons fired during my time.

When I was born housewives were doing what they'd been doing since time began, and things didn't change drastically until the early 1960s. No preceding decades brought so many changes to any species as the last pair have to women.

Since Eve told Adam, "Try it. You'll like it," women had spent their lives caring for men, their dwellings and their children. Only the tools changed. The bunch of twigs which swept the cave gave way to the electric broom, but women were still wielding the handle. The animal roasting over an open fire gave way to the microwave oven, but women were still being blamed for burning the roast. White cotton diapers gave way to Pampers, but women were still scraping revolting gook from small bottoms.

When doctors wore painted masks, when architects lugged boulders, when druggists were alchemists and newscasters were still town criers, housewives were doing what they're doing today. Or rather, what they were doing yesterday. For in 1979 everything is changing and nothing will ever be the same again.

Being involved in any revolution can make day-to-day living a bit of a strain. But when the issue at stake is the removal of the very core of your life, the strain snowballs into a trauma. If life is a game, then women of my generation are the first ones ever forced to play with constantly changing rules. All these changes are supposed to be for the best, to make the game more fair and more fun. But it doesn't always work out that way. The game has gotten more complicated, old rules are dropped slowly while new ones are added with alarming regularity.

Having struggled for our rights, we ended up adding to our responsibilities. Feminists must be applauded for fighting for our options, but they haven't told us how to deal with them. We are encouraged to assume more duties, but not to drop the old ones. Women my age were raised one way, then told to behave another. Is it any wonder we're all reaching for Geritol? Or gin? Or both?

Twenty-two years ago, when I had our first child, if I'd decided to put him into the care of a sitter and go back to work, my family would have gone into shock. My parents would have insisted I get psychiatric help. My in-laws would have chipped in to pay for it. My aunts would have hyperventilated from gasping and Grandma would have taken a swipe at me with her cane to bring me to my senses.

Today when a woman has a baby and quits her job to care for it *she* is suspect. What is she trying to prove? Is she perhaps a case of arrested development because she wants to play dolls when she should be playing store? What kind of an egomaniac wants her baby to be totally dependent on her? Or worse yet, what kind of monster would try to raise a child to have her values?

It's impossible to figure out how things turned around so quickly, even recognizing that great change came about with advancements in birth control. Married women began planning their families, arranging to have babies at convenient times during vacations or semester breaks. And not having babies every year for four straight years like one dumb bunny I used to know.

But the working part still mystifies me. How did working become so important that no baby was permitted to interrupt even the most mundane job? When Margaret Sanger fought for voluntary motherhood, she believed that babies would be valued more when they were born the fruit of deep yearning instead of the result of ignorance or accident. She believed that only when motherhood became a question of free choice could it be truly sacred. It hasn't worked out that way. Never in history have more babies been conceived by design and never has motherhood been more undervalued.

Most of the women in my generation who have families sought jobs out of pressing financial necessity and then only after their children hit school age. Other women my age went back to school or off to work out of sheer desperation. Many of them had moved to the suburbs, away from families and old friends, and the privacy they sought turned out to be more like isolation. In all the years past a woman who owned a large house was never expected to stay in it alone all day. She had a hired girl or a spinster sister or her mother to provide another pair of hands, some help with the babies. But these new suburban women were alone. Grandmothers who traditionally had provided the best day care were far away (or taking scuba lessons). The hired girl had been hired by a corporation offering a pension plan and spinster sisters had become swinging singles.

This modern housewife was further isolated by her own affluence. With her color-coordinated washer and dryer she had no need to run down to the stream and beat clothes on the rocks with the other women or even to hang out the window pinning wet laundry on the clothesline and chatting with the neighbors à la Molly Goldberg. With her fifteen-cubic-foot freezer she didn't have to go marketing every day and with her imitation-wood-paneled station wagon she had no occasion to even bump into a friend on the street.

Her suburban husband wasn't much help. He faced long and exhausting commutation and rarely was up to waltzing through the door at night like Fred Astaire, there to light up her evening with amusing patter and romance. His precious spare time was spent battling crabgrass and clogged septics. He took up do-it-yourselfing to accomplish needed repairs and improvements and spent an inordinate number of Saturday afternoons in the local hospital emergency room.

With children in school all day, her husband coming home nights late and weary and spending his weekends getting tetanus shots, the suburban housewife started to itch, then twitch. Going back to college or out to work often seemed the only solution to her relentless boredom. One of my friends frankly admits she looked for a job out of sheer loneliness and refers to her expensive development as a classy displaced-persons camp.

Then, too, working became fashionable. Women's liberation was in flower and on every front we were assaulted with the glories of doing your own thing. We were urged to throw off our aprons, unfasten our bras, pull on support hose and lurch out into the labor force. Every medium chimed in. Television commercials began using lines like, "With my job, I don't have time for windows" and "Honey, how do you do it? With the house, the kids and your job, how do you have such young-looking hands?"

Situation comedies changed. Today Lucy and Ethel would have jobs and the jokes would involve putting things over on bosses instead of husbands. Shows like *Father Knows Best* and *Leave it to Beaver* were replaced by one-parent families, and Doris Day and Julia, Mrs. Partridge and then Alice made working widowhood look like such a lark it's a wonder we didn't all start mixing ground glass in our husbands' hamburgers.

Ladies' magazines, whose fiction had most often portrayed a woman's realization that what she really wanted was a husband, home and baby-makes-three, began running stories about self-fulfillment, picturing heroines who combined motherhood with a career. They also had article upon article on the joys of working and made it look like a piece of cake. We read about all these women who had successful careers, homes and families, and some of the lives pictured stagger the imagination.

Ms. Priscilla Perfect maintains an immaculate house, has two A-student children and a full-time job as a marine biologist (note photograph of her at work wearing her size-six bikini). She plays third viola in the local symphony and devotes much of her spare time to her poetry group. She and her husband (a Tyrone Power look-alike) enjoy entertaining their multitude of friends at elegant gourmet dinners. And she jogs three miles every morning. (Want to bet she also sends Christmas letters?)

Working became so stylish that for the first time in anyone's memory rich women began taking jobs. Not satisfied to be patrons of the arts or do volunteer work among the less fortunate, they wanted paychecks to reassure them of their value. I keep one article, "Beautiful People Who Work," on the shelf in the bathroom. In case I ever swallow poison I can read a few lines and be sure to throw up. This article recounted the trials and obstacles several courageous ladies overcame on their way to fulfilling careers. My favorite was an automobile heiress who's now into designing clothes and facing the same problems as all working women. She said she's found the pressure of taking care of the kids—while the nurse is on vacation—and getting to the office can give her moments when she feels "like packing it all in and going to Payne Whitney." Poor baby! When questioned about designing clothes for average women when she was hardly one herself, she replied in no uncertain terms that, "We lived like everyone else in Grosse Pointe." About the only thing she left out was, "Let them eat cake."

Working is *in*. Mrs. Onassis is doing it. Her sister the princess from Poland is doing it. And they make it look so appealing. But when my fellow housewives started working, all they discovered were new depths of meaning to the word "exhausted." One woman wrote saying her job had become a "guilt trip. . . . I've become a slipshod mother, a neurotic wife, a rotten homemaker and an overtired lover." Maybe she should try Payne Whitney.

I was most surprised at how many working mothers wrote saying that they were reluctant to leave their children and homes but were pressured to get jobs by husbands wanting added income, a bigger car or house. In most cases the husband had sworn to share the housework and child care fifty-fifty and in most cases he hadn't hit ten-ninety. That brings up catch twenty-three. This liberation is terrific for the career girl who finds increased opportunities, but it's a mixed blessing to the working mother who was usually brought up to assume full responsibility for homemaking but now feels expected to take a job. Her husband expects her to help out financially, but was brought up to consider homemaking "women's work." So these mothers are stuck with being working women plus doing women's work. And that's called "liberation."

I know a couple who work in the same office, commute together, and when they walk into their house at night he slumps in his chair, turns on the TV and asks, "What's for dinner?" Women can tell themselves that a clean, neat house is unimportant and attempt to acquire their husband's laissez-faire attitude toward dust and debris. But when a guest drops by, the wife feels compelled to apologize for the mess. Even the most liberated mother will feel guilt if she accepts a job any distance from her home and children, while never questioning her husband's long commute.

Husbands and wives of the future will handle things better because they won't have preconceived notions of roles to deal with and will have different expectations. Even today's young husbands are more educated and conditioned to share things with their wives. One of the most graphic examples of this is the husband's participation in childbirth, the original "women's work."

For centuries, in almost every culture, women gave birth assisted by other women, and men were delighted with the arrangement. When Grandma went into labor, Grandpa would take the trolley to the end of the line. I remember Dad sitting in the farthest corner of the fathers' lounge holding *Time* magazine upside down. My own husband had no desire to see his children come into the world. He said paying the hospital bill was enough participation for him. It just seems so ironic that couples today who demand to see their children born will so often hand them over to strangers to be raised.

I opted for *un*natural childbirth myself, but I've

heard the stories. And Lord help me, even seen the pictures. But the most unique reaction I ever heard came from a cousin in Ireland who'd watched his baby being born. Said he, "It was very strange. You're used to seeing a person come through a door. And you're used to seeing a person get out of a car. But *that's* just not a place you're used to seeing a person come out of."

CHAPTER

THE WOMEN'S MOVEMENT HAS DONE MORE TO GIVE housekeeping a bad name than Rebecca's Mrs. Danvers. But that's not the only thing that irritates. I also have problems with the word "liberation." Why not "equality"? I have fantasized about space creatures hovering overhead, picking up radio signals that spell out the oppression of women, demanding their liberation. As the creatures come closer, for encounters of a second kind, they will observe humans dressed in suits, carrying briefcases, pushing onto commuter trains and smaller humans waving good-bye and heading home for a cup of coffee. They will see humans hauling crates on a dock in freezing wind while other smaller humans sit at desks in warm offices typing. And the space creatures, having exalted intelligence, will conclude that the larger creatures are the women and definitely require liberation.

Besides the semantics, it seems fair to question the kind of woman who claims to speak for all women. We see no man purporting to speak for all men, but from every corner women spring up who feel that merely sharing anatomical traits qualifies them to know all women's needs and to tell us what's best for us whether we want it or not—a hypothesis once exclusive to the Jesuits.

These well-meaning ladies are quick to tell us what to do today, but give scant attention to our tomorrows. They lay before us all the goodies we deserve to have, but neglect to mention the price we'll have to pay.

Betty Friedan, Germaine Greer, Kate Millett, Gloria Steinem, etc., are extremely intelligent women, writing and lecturing about their feelings and hopes, but they don't reflect mine. It could be because they are committed intellectuals, educated at Smith and Cambridge, who majored in esoteric subjects while I went to Pratt Institute and took home economics. That they are orchids; I'm a daisy. That they're ripe Brie and Château Rothschild while I'm Velveeta and Boones' Farm. If their gifts are too sublime to be wasted in a kitchen or nursery, mine are just right. And I believe there are greater numbers of women like me than like them. Not that we are more dimwitted or obtuse than they, for high I.Q. is no guarantee of sensitivity (or intelligence for that matter). We just have different needs and values.

Mama's Aunt Molly sold dresses during the Kennedy administration and complained that her customers wanted to dress like Jackie but were built more like Eleanor. Life-styles like dress styles are too often set by the extraordinary or even the bizarre, and we women, craving style and acceptance, follow like sheep.

Ms. Greer writes of the middle-class myth of love and marriage, but I cannot imagine women of any class relating to her idea of child rearing, which is to bear a child outside of marriage and send it to a child farm to be raised. The mother's sole responsibility would be financial and she would be known to her child as "womb mother," an infrequent visitor who avoids imposing her values on him.

I am too hopelessly bourgeois to bear a child just to send it away. How many women surrender babies for adoption only to spend their lives searching for them? They're undoubtedly middle class too. Or maybe they're just normal women following their most basic natural instincts.

Ms. Greer claims it is a loss that the more educated and intelligent women, reluctant to be tied down by marriage and a home, are not reproducing and the world is poorer for it. Perhaps, but most of us in there having babies who aren't so highbrow may make better mothers. We may even manage, as her middle-class parents did, to occasionally produce a superior child.

Ms. Friedan, herself a caring mother (and in fact one of the few mothers in the front ranks of the movement), is less radical. She does persist though in urging women out of the house whether or not they have anywhere to go. She also neglects to offer solutions to the dilemma this flight from home engenders. Clearly, it is beneath anyone's dignity to clean another person's toilet, but someone has to do it. Obviously, no one can find intellectual stimulation in changing a foul diaper, but someone must do it. And we can't always count on feeble-minded girls and eight-year-olds.

Ms. Steinem is a remarkably attractive woman who moves in very sophisticated circles and, although I admire her social conscience and her devotion to equality of opportunity, I don't feel she can relate to me. Ms. Millett is an avowed lesbian and clearly has different needs. Yet these are the women whose opinions and values are being taught in our universities. Books reflecting their radical ideas dominate college reading lists, while true academic freedom should insist that students have some exposure to other viewpoints.

Anne Morrow Lindbergh beautifully articulates a different philosophy, but her name has never appeared on any women's studies book list that I've seen. My own patron saint, Phyllis McGinley, won a Pulitzer prize for her writing and had well-defined thoughts on women's roles, but her works are never referred to. Obviously, some balance is required, for radical feminists don't always have all the answers for all their sisters.

Shaw (G. B., not Irwin) said that a rebel has an obligation to replace the conventions he destroys with better ones. Ms. Friedan and her accomplices offer no sensible alternatives. The self-appointed leaders of the women's movement, like most revolutionaries, have little appetite for rebuilding crumbling structures after the dust has settled. Yet we are directed to follow them, to swallow their theories whole, and to hesitate is to be considered weak. To question is to be judged ignorant.

My husband once took a math course taught by a very formidable Japanese professor who started off by announcing that he welcomed questions. Then he added, "But please never to ask *stupid* questions." Would you dare raise your hand after that?

But we must question even if we appear stupid or,

God forbid, old-fashioned. Liberation from child care may or may not be better for women, but it cannot be judged better for society. Families are breaking apart at an alarming rate. Juvenile delinquency is rampant. Vandalism by middle-class youngsters is pandemic. Educational standards are eroding and some of the current morality would make Nero blush.

Many women who are finding themselves are also finding heart disease, high blood pressure, ulcers and withering loneliness. Whatever else women are getting out of their liberation and self-fulfillment, they are not necessarily happier.

Only an idiot would suggest that women revert to second-class status, but must children pay the price for their mother's freedom? Would it so damage a woman's career opportunities to spend a few years giving her child a healthy start in life? Because home-making was wrong for some women yesterday, is it unthinkable for all women today? Must it be all or nothing? Can't we attempt moderation? (Now there's a word you don't often see these days.)

It wouldn't be easy. Today extremism is the norm instead of the exception. Everything and everyone is *in* or *out*. And homemaking is labeled *out*. And what's really *in* are labels.

I could never forget the mortification I felt when I wore new shoes to a dance and my date pointed out that the price was still stuck on the soles. Occasionally, wearing a new dress, one tag would be overlooked and you could have fainted from embarrassment. Today, labels are what you buy and what you show most proudly. Everything is monogrammed, but not with *your* initials. I have a rich cousin who's very into Givenchy and you'd think her clothes were all hand-me-downs from Greta Garbo. The best-dressed women are no more than walking billboards. They are sporting message-bearing T-shirts, often vastly more amusing than the lady wearing them.

Not content to let our clothes tell where we're at, we plaster our automobiles with labels that define us further. It's possible to tell more about a person by looking at his car than by tapping his phone: national origins, political persuasion, marriage encounter, vacation locales and values systems ("I Brake For Animals." Does that mean he barrels over children and cripples?). I hesitate to blow my horn as warning to a fellow motorist lest I be perceived to share his religion or be sex-starved.

Our society's morbid preoccupation with labels carries over into the women's movement. If you hesitate to buy women's lib one hundred percent, then surely you must be a disciple of Mrs. Schlafly or a follower of Mrs. Morgan. It was revealing that so many women who wrote to me said that if I was starting an organization, they wanted to join; for we middle-of-the-roaders find ourselves without a label and therefore without any status.

Like so many other women, I just can't find a comfortable niche. Having taken forty-five years to begin to know what's right for me, I am staggered by Phyllis Schlafly's certain knowledge of what's right for everyone. And as a person who hesitates to recommend a doctor, or even a restaurant, to someone else, I am awed by a woman who feels qualified to tell other women how to live their lives. She reminds me of Dad's Aunt Cora, who Mama claimed was "often in error but never in doubt."

Marabel Morgan's philosophy is shared by many women who testify that her approach saved their marriages and enriched their lives, and I applaud her attitude in looking for the good points in our loved ones and not dwelling on the bad. One friend who had a very traumatic childhood says his mother constantly criticized his father. She went so far as to take her children for Sunday strolls through nicer neighborhoods, pointing out lovely houses where "you'd all be living if your father were a better man." That attitude, though extreme, is not terribly uncommon.

But for my tastes, Mrs. Morgan goes too far. The idea of husband as hero and wife as cheerleader (complete with short skirt and boots) seems to offend women and insult men. To use sex to get what you want is demeaning to both parties. It is more important that married people be good friends, and friends do not manipulate each other. They are honest. If I don't tell my husband the speech he's planning for the Rotary is a stinker, who will? And if he doesn't tell me my new red-and-blue tweed outfit makes me look like the purple people-eater, who will? (The kids—that's who.)

Mrs. Morgan has developed a "Total Woman" course and one of its requirements is that you must initiate sex with your husband every night for a week. Won't he be flattered to learn he's being lusted after only as part of a homework assignment?

The idea of fawning over your husband, playing the

obsequious slave to his macho master, is just too phony and contrived. I personally couldn't keep a straight face. She does though make a valid point about appearing relaxed and attractive when your husband comes home at night. That's something I always mean to do, but I lose track of time and usually end up greeting my husband looking like I just fell off a runaway horse.

I have an old friend down south who took the Total Woman course without telling her husband, and he was immensely relieved when he discovered the cause of her suddenly attentive behavior. He said he'd concluded that either she had a lover or he had only weeks to live.

CHAPTER

6

As a young woman in the early 1950s, the only times I ever heard mention of a woman's movement was when she was discussing irregularity. That was an uncomplicated time when women's roles were not yet hyphenated: when she was a housewife or career girl but seldom both; when motherhood was considered a full-time, lifetime job and morality was black and white with few gray areas; when even our vices were clearly categorized (in my case, mortal or venial).

Most of us who married in the fifties were squares and conformists. It's fashionable today to knock the Eisenhower years as dull and unimaginative, but it must have been a grand time to be a parent.

We, however, hit our stride as parents in the 1960s. And women who had been brought up to value acceptance watched their children protesting everything. These flower children cared deeply about redwoods and baby seals while inflicting great anguish on their parents, accusing them of bourgeois values while living off their hard-earned monies. Women who seldom left the house without gloves and dress shields saw their daughters going out barefoot and braless.

Parents who'd dreamed of their daughter being married in the family church found themselves standing on a windy beach, watching her tie the knot with some bearded drifter while balancing on a slippery rock in the California surf; both of them dressed in Mexican shirts and jeans patched in the most unfortunate places. And precariously sharing the rock with a self-anointed minister wearing a Nehru suit and a ponytail. Instead of the traditional bouquet, the bride was carrying their first grandchild (a.k.a. love child) who would be born weeks later and named Sunflower or Peaceable Twilight.

Families who treasured homes and roots saw their children floating around the country in campers and rusty old buses. That always amused me because I remember Grandma had a picture over her mantel in Brooklyn of a lovely thatched cottage which she said reminded her of her girlhood home in County Cavan. So, years later when my parents visited Ireland, they went searching for that house. They drove to the small village, found a very old man who remembered Grandma's family, and Mama asked him to point out the house. He chuckled and said, "Bless your foolish head, girl. The house went with them." It had been no more than a shanty and had collapsed as soon as they abandoned it.

The irony of it all. After the sacrifice Grandma made to have her own house (attached though it was to its neighbors), and the effort that went into educating her children so that they might have proper houses surrounded by lawns, there were her grandchildren back living in houses that went with them.

We were relieved to see the 1960s pass. We'd had our fill of Vietnam, assassination and rioting, of new morality, protesting and long hair. Little did we know what we were headed for in the 1970s.

Protesting died out and the war ended, campuses quieted down, haircuts ceased to be considered a crime against nature, but the so-called new morality hung on. Couples who'd never known unmarried sex watched with bewilderment at the carryings-on of their teen-age children. Bewilderment often mixed with envy. As one of my uncles put it, "Why did the sexual revolution have to come just as I was running out of ammunition?"

Besides the new morality, there were other less-dramatic holdovers from the sixties. The youth culture hung on and after centuries where youngsters tried to look grown-up, now adults were trying to pass for teen-agers. Instead of the daughter sneaking Mom's fur jacket, Mom was pinching the daughter's jeans and T-shirts. *Vogue* magazine had unceremoniously dumped Mrs. Exeter.

We even imitated our children's speech and picked up their expressions—albeit always lagging behind. My sons had a coach who was so determined to be "with it" that he took to using all the slang expressions, but he never got them right. He'd say things like, "That's out of state" or "Right arm, brother, right arm."

A reverse snobbery took hold. After centuries where the wealthy set styles for the masses to follow, the cycle suddenly reversed. The most affluent people began dressing like sharecroppers. The man in the gray flannel suit was going to his Madison Avenue office

73

in denims. Wealthy women bought expensive pre-faded pre-patched jeans. Or ethnic outfits.

I vividly remember the night about eight years ago, soon after my last child was born, when I found myself walking into a party wearing my trusty black dress and pearls and being panic-stricken as I saw the other guests and realized it must be a costume party and I hadn't gotten the message. It wasn't one at all. I was hopelessly out of place, but the other ladies (a very artsy bunch) were all doing their things dressed as Navahos, Hindus, Himalayans and Polynesians. And when I say they were letting it all hang out, I mean exactly that. Between my black dress and my nursing bra, Queen Victoria couldn't have been more of a sore thumb.

My husband was equally conspicuous in a shirt, tie and jacket, for all of the other men were in tight denim outfits or pastel polyester suits with flowered shirts opened halfway down to reveal pie-shaped wedges of their flabby gray-haired chests. Several of the men were wearing more jewelry than I own and it became clear that male menopause was soaring toward new heights.

The changing dress styles were an important part of the times because although sex was *in*, sexist was *out*. The new liberated woman no longer wanted to be thought of as a sex object, and I don't blame her, even though I had no solid experience being so regarded. It is demeaning for a woman to be hooted at on the street by construction gangs and to have to run around the desk pursued by a panting employer.

One of my best friends had a mastectomy and soon

afterward switched jobs. Her new boss made several blatant passes at her and managed to brush his hand against her chest every time he handed her something. She finally became so incensed that when he'd made a particularly overt grab at her right breast, she reached inside her dress, pulled out her prosthesis and handed it to him, suggesting that since he was so fond of squeezing it he might want to keep it in his coat pocket for constant availability. He never bothered her again.

Feminists began to regard any reference to their sexuality as evidence of male chauvinism and a man trying to compliment an attractive woman had a real predicament. Men were used to telling women they had beautiful eyes and terrific figures, but soon learned instead to express admiration for their ladylove's grasp of Middle Eastern politics or her longshoreman's hook.

What did present a contradiction in all this rejection of sexism was that the catalogs from the most sedate department stores began offering the kind of lingerie that was once only available in plain brown wrappers from Frederick's of Hollywood. I never thought I'd see the day my teen-age sons would be fighting over the pictures in Bloomingdale's flyers.

The sexual revolution continued unabated. Marriage went out and living together came in. Now your living arrangements are your business and I know unwed couples who treat each other more kindly than the legally tied. But we've got to find a word for it. The whole thing becomes too awkward when you try to introduce "my daughter Jill and her roommate Jack." One of Mama's old friends refers to "my granddaughter Mary and her escort John."

Sex changes became more common and here again there are problems with semantics. One neighbor whose son became her daughter says she's accepting it pretty well, knowing the heartache that forced the decision. What's bothering her now, besides the constant borrowing of her best clothes, are the pronouns: "She's so slim now, you'd hardly believe he was such a fat baby"; "She's a wonderful doctor, and why not when he had such fine training as an intern."

To digress for a minute, have you ever noticed that in the world of words, pronouns are the real troublemakers? How many fights centered around *his* paycheck and *her* bills? We know our child is in trouble when his father comes home and says, "Where is *your* son?" And we can foresee weeks of hostility when a husband playing at the net hears the tennis ball whiz by his head and shouts to his wife, "*Yours.*"

Back to the sexual revolution. It wouldn't have been quite so traumatic if it hadn't been accompanied by the disappearance from our language of that lovely old word, "discretion." No one uses it anymore. We are fed more information about people's sex lives than we could possibly find interesting. Why must everyone know everyone else's sexual practices and preferences? It makes no difference to me whether my child is taught math by a heterosexual teacher or a lesbian teacher as long as she is a good teacher. I would not be the least bit reluctant to be saved from a burning building by a gay fireman or protected from a mugger by a gay cop. Why should it matter to society what a person does in his bedroom? I, and it's a personal thing, I know, am much more offended by the guy with the loud transistor radio sitting beside me on a bus than I am by the guy on the other side wearing earrings.

It is absurd for sexual preferences to have any part in employment. All this affirmative action to assure balance has gone too far. It's one thing to have a proportionate number of women or minorities, but where do you stop with sexual preferences? After establishing quotas for homosexuals, do you then apportion the heterosexual jobs among sadomasochists, foot fetishers, etc.? Or, if we are going to dismiss people for "socially unacceptable sexual inclinations," will we also dismiss wife beaters, child abusers, reckless drivers, tax dodgers, alcoholics and pot smokers? And watch our economy grind to a halt. How much more sensible to simply require that every person holding a job be qualified to perform it!

When this new sexual openness and experimentation became mixed with the kiss-and-tell syndrome, we began to hear wild stories about sex in the suburbs. I just want to know, where? I mean I guess it's there, but I'm not benefiting personally and frankly wouldn't know where to start. My meter reader is past the retirement age and so short of wind he hardly makes it back up the cellar stairs. My plumber will never see sixty again and his ticker is so bad I have to carry his toolbox in from the truck. The exterminator probably has a beautiful soul, but he's been around rodents so long he looks like Ben walking on his hind legs.

And if I were to find some Adonis who was interested, I'd have to find a place to go with him. I mean just the arrangements, finding time between the children's dental appointments and cheerleading practice, his car or mine and if mine, how do I get all those McDonald's wrappers cleared away without inviting suspicion? I would have heartburn and a migraine just from the planning, and if I ever went through with it I'd spend the next decade watching for a scarlet A to surface on my forehead.

It's a moot point anyway, for I find that when a man draws me aside to whisper something in my ear, invariably he's vainly hoping my husband will fix his speeding ticket or that I'll give his wife my soda bread recipe.

But while I am not personally involved in the sexual revolution, I nevertheless find myself inundated with all the attendant information. For nowhere in our society has the lack of moderation and discretion been more obvious than in the area of sex. And while knowledge of sex is important and necessary, it's now a question of overkill. Sex has become downright boring because, as Voltaire pointed out, the secret of being tiresome is to tell everything.

We not only know more about Farrah and the Super Bowl than we ever wanted to know, but about sex and perversion as well. Today, anything worth doing is worth overdoing. If five months of baseball was good, seven months must be better. I'm old enough to remember when hockey was a winter sport and Thanksgiving meant turkey and the last football game of the season. Now the latter comes in mid-January and, invariably, is itself a turkey.

A good book becomes a movie. A book is then written about the making of the movie. Then a sequel to the book comes along which is made into a sequel of the movie and the cycle continues *ad infinitum*. Writers' heaven must be full of authors kicking themselves because they didn't think to do *Son of David Copperfield* or *Canterbury Tales—Part II*.

Overkill extends to every facet of our lives and being overinformed becomes a mixed blessing. Our grandparents had the other extreme because they were uninformed about many things, but primarily sex. Not that my generation was so smart. My cousin Betsy told me all her mother ever said to her about sex was, "Do you know where babies come from?" She said she did, and her mother's reply was, "Good. Now don't have any." In his autobiography, Peter Ustinov tells of going to a boys' prep school in England where the sex education consisted of a pamphlet that began, "You may have noticed between your legs . . ."

At least he got a pamphlet. Most of us picked up our muddled knowledge from the street kids who claimed (inaccurately) to know it all. Our friend Mac recently told us that his eighth-grade classmate, Ziggy, who was their resident expert, once bragged that he'd had sex with Sadie and took her cherry. Mac was in awe and asked how he could be sure. Ziggy leered knowingly and said, "I saw it fall out and roll across the floor."

Ziggy notwithstanding, we were still way ahead of our grandparents. I remember Grandma asking Mama if having a hysterectomy meant she'd have trouble getting pregnant. Grandma knew how babies got started and how they were born, but what happened in between was a bigger mystery than the trinity. Such ignorance seems incredible, but you have to realize that Grandma's seven children were delivered by a Mrs. Murphy, who also cooked and cleaned for ten days afterward and had a package rate of twenty-five dollars.

And I wouldn't say Grandma was skeptical about doctors, but I vividly recall the day I brought my first-born home from the hospital. She took one look at the untidy condition of his navel and said, "The Indians did a better job with their teeth."

Our teen-age children know things our grandparents never imagined. A neighbor who's been married over fifty years confided that she'd read *The Joy of Sex* but hid it from her husband because he'd be so upset if he ever found out what he'd missed.

The sexual openness often makes me uncomfortable because there are some things I'd just rather not know —and other people's bowel problems and sexual proclivities are high on the list. But my older friends and neighbors are befuddled by it all. One of them was stunned when a roomful of people laughed after she'd told them her hairdresser gave a great blow job. And you may find this hard to believe, but I have an aunt who threw up in the movie aisle when she went to see *Deep Throat*, because she thought it was about Vaughn Monroe.

CHAPTER

IN YET ANOTHER IRONIC TWIST, JUST AS SEX BECAME
easily available and socially acceptable, many
women began turning against men. In the pro-
longed struggle for equality, men had somehow become the adversaries and to socialize with them was
tantamount to fraternization with the enemy. To marry
one might be perceived as outright collaboration.

That attitude may be partly responsible for the ap-
parent increase in lesbianism. And while some of my
best friends are women, I don't want my daughter to
marry one. Because the gay life isn't. One of the finest
women I've ever known is a lesbian, but her life has
been one long heartache, clouded by ridicule and rejection. And social acceptance which might have accompanied the more flexible morality has been tragically
mitigated by a new wave of cruel anti-homosexual
sentiment.

Why the women's movement has fostered a rejection
of men and often seems to view them as antagonists
is difficult for me as a mother to understand, since
each man was borne by a woman, raised by her and
profoundly influenced by her. Have we so failed with

our sons that they have grown up into greedy oppressors?

In the long history of this world there have always been men who exploited women and women who exploited men. If marriage was unfair to women, it was also unfair to men. And life was usually unfair to them both.

We women have legitimate grievances, but to blame men for the ills of the world is stupid. There has been no emergence of political Camelots since women won the franchise. As citizens sharing equal votes we have proved ourselves to be just as unimaginative and noble, as self-serving and altruistic as men. As world leaders we have been no more effective or uncorrupt than men. In the business world we are often quick to assume the same values and tactics we abhor in men.

The basic flaw in this anti-men attitude is that women are the only minority that is thoroughly integrated. No apartheid or segregation has ever been possible. Men are our fathers and brothers, our lovers and husbands, our sons and grandsons. Our lives are intertwined and whatever problems we have must be solved by men and women working together with mutual respect and goodwill.

One imposing weakness of the 1977 Houston conference was the exclusion of large numbers of men. Until then, the main thrust of the women's movement seemed to be equality with men, an equality that demanded that men assume their share of responsibility in sexual and family matters. Right *arm!* It was about time we put an end to men complaining about the hardship they experienced when their wives "got pregnant."

Since pregnancy is not a self-inflicted condition, it is proper that men share in its implications. And since a child has two parents, his care should be of equal concern to both.

But at Houston, the movement took an about-face as issue after issue was treated as a "woman's problem." Although it's her body that is involved, abortion is not just a woman's concern. She was impregnated by a man, usually by a man who cares deeply about her, most often her husband. The conception of their unwanted baby is not just her problem, any more than the day care of their children should be just her problem.

Excluding men also seems a mistake because it just isn't enough for *women*'s attitudes to alter. Men's attitudes toward our aspirations must also change, be more positive and supportive. It would have done small good for blacks to proclaim their equality as long as whites were unwilling to acknowledge it. Equality results not from how you perceive yourself but how you are regarded by others. Even the most radical black activist would concede that whatever steps have been taken toward racial equality were substantially aided by the encouragement and participation of white people who supported their cause.

But at Houston, as at most feminist conclaves, too much emphasis was put on the few issues that divide women, like abortion and lesbianism, and not those they might all agree on and rally together for, like Social Security for homemakers and fair pension rights for women. While feminists expend their energies on the semantics of "chairpersons" and "girls," the practical problems are left unattended.

We need equality with men. We don't need to be treated like men. If they don't attempt to infiltrate the ladies' sodality or Hadassah, why do we need to integrate men's bars and the Rotary? Personally, I have always felt that next to first crack at the lifeboats, one of the biggest things women had going for them was never having to sit through a Rotary luncheon.

For many of us, the most towering achievement of the women's movement to date has been the repeal of pay toilets. There is an army of middle-aged and older women in this country who might sign on with the movement if it pledged itself to a better image for women than that provided by advertisers of feminine hygiene sprays and the producers of *Charlie's Angels*. Sexist advertisements are as offensive to conservative women as they are to radicals. Sensitive maternity care is important to every pregnant woman, whatever her background or politics. Feminist preoccupation with narrow, divisive issues has only served to hurt the cause of all women.

Our goals, however just and virtuous, will not be achieved by strident and abrasive leaders. In selling this nation, men and women, the idea of female equality, the selection of Bella Abzug as chairperson of a media event like the Houston conference was at best a public relations disaster and at worst a devious attempt to sabotage E.R.A. Especially when there were other women, Millicent Fenwick or Ella Grasso, for instance, who might have impressed the unconvinced majority with the dignity and nobility of their cause.

Mrs. Abzug is an accomplished politician whose

integrity is irreproachable. But however great her devotion to feminism, she is not the proper image to sell the idea of women's rights (or even toothpaste) to a skeptical public. Her heart may be in the right place, but she has the regal bearing of a roller derby queen combined with the subtle approach of a McCormick reaper.

The failure of E.R.A. to pass is a tribute to how out of touch feminist leaders have become. The stumbling block to ratification is not the chauvinism of men but the resistance of the majority of women who feel alienated from a movement that appears contemptuous of their values and goals.

You would never believe it watching the goings-on at Houston, but most women agree on most things. We all want equal opportunity and equal pay. We all want better control over our own destinies. We all think every baby has a right to life—to a decent, hunger-free, meaningful life. We all agree that abortion is not a desirable thing and that, ideally, unwanted babies should never be conceived. We all want better education and medical care for our children and we want to see our grandchildren come into a world free from war, starvation and poverty. And we all want to be treated with respect; not to be put down because of our sex, our color, our life-style or our profession. Or lack of one.

Part of the problem is that in seeking equality with men, we too often are encouraged to act like men. We are told that the traditional female qualities of compassion and sympathy are signs of weakness. It is suggested that the very roles we enjoyed most and those that gave us the greatest satisfaction are now an anathema to any intelligent female. And that to compete with men, we must become less feminine. But what about the balance of nature and the theory that the two sexes were created to complement each other? If there were no differences, nature would not have arranged that every child require a parent of each sex, and men might bear babies and women grow beards. Attempting to deny sexual differences constitutes affront to women. Our qualities are too unique, our gifts too sublime, to content ourselves with being nothing more than smaller, weaker versions of men.

Today it is almost perceived as an insult if you describe a woman as feminine. In fact that word is most often used pejoratively to describe weak men. Persons of both sexes intending to compliment a woman will say, "She plays tennis like a man" or "she thinks like a man." How stupid. They'd never say, "He plays bridge like a woman," unless they intended ridicule. I don't want to do anything like a man except maybe to have use of that convenient plumbing, such a handy thing to have at a picnic.

This whole great nonsense with "chairpersons" is silly. What's wrong with "chairwoman"? Is the word "woman" offensive or degrading? An inner-city hospital maternity clinic actually has a sign: "This lounge reserved for pregnant persons." Now look at the way blacks handle their push for equality. Instead of attempting to emulate whites and minimize racial differences, they declared, "Black is beautiful." Rather than straighten their hair, they pointed up their uniqueness with marvelous Afro hairdos (and looked so terrific that white women are paying big bucks to have their hair frizzed). The blacks take pride in being different. No claim is made to being better than anyone else—special but equal. The women's movement should make as much sense.

Much importance is placed on eliminating sexual differences, but to obliterate differences is to dilute life. Irish and Italians are different. Orientals and Caucasians are different. In many ways all are similar, but it is our differences that make us interesting. We can praise and cling to diversity without sacrificing equality. Equality should never demand sameness.

Men and women *are* different. When, after three sons, I had my first daughter, Grandma told me, "You'll see there's no such thing as a little girl, they're just short women. Just like there's no such thing as a grown man, they're just tall boys." And I've found it to be absolutely true.

A brother might say little girls tend to be manipulative and calculating, but I prefer realistic and resourceful. Phyllis McGinley says it best in a poem which describes children finding out that there is no Santa Claus. The little boys feel resentful and duped and run to tell their parents they're on to them. Thereby setting themselves up for meager loot.

> But little girls no blinder
> When faced by mortal fact
> Are cleverer and kinder
> And brimming full of tact.
> Agnostics born but Bernhardts bred,
> They hang their stockings by the bed,

For little girls can draw conclusions
And profit from their lost illusions.

(Like Grandma said, short women.)

I had four younger brothers and four even younger sons, so I've spent my life surrounded by males. And I would never suggest that grown men are immature or childlike, but they are often tall boys. Their games remain important to them long after they've established important careers. There's a plaque available in gift shops that reads, "The only difference between men and boys is the price of their toys." How many women who make money go off to buy sailboats or racing cars? And can you even imagine a mature woman who's just achieved a milestone in her career, celebrating by having champagne poured over her head?

The longer I live, the more I respect women—their ability to handle life, to face adversity. Most men are devastated by losing their fortunes while their wives make accommodations and adjustments. Widows almost always are able to deal with their plight better than widowers. Women accept pain as part of life while men cry out in protest. Women have a gift for seeing the total picture, for being able to appreciate the good things while coping with the bad. And the female of the species may be deadlier than the male, but she can cook a simple meal without using every pot in the kitchen.

While most firmly believing in women, it seems ridiculous to suggest that they should be encouraged to do all the things that men do and vice versa. No woman should ever be denied the right to any job she honestly feels she wants, but once again a little common sense is indicated. Equal opportunity for all is an admirable goal, but it sometimes gets ludicrous, for certain jobs require specific physical abilities. Two English comedians do a sketch about a one-legged man auditioning for the role of Tarzan. After trying several subtle kinds of discouragement, the frustrated casting director finally cries, "Look, I have nothing against your right leg, but neither does your right leg."

There are specific jobs certain types of people do best and no matter how much I read about men sharing housework and doing it well, I remain unconvinced. The idea of men and women dividing the chores around the house sounds feasible, but it just won't work because men are constitutionally unable to do housework. Not physically but emotionally, for men need constant encouragement and housework, like virtue, is its own reward.

My sons, like most teen-age boys, love to eat and took up cooking when they realized that was the only way they'd ever have a cheesecake all to themselves or a whole batch of chili to pig out on. Every so often they cook for the family or make a special treat and here's where their need for encouragement surfaces.

I often cook four-course meals, spending hours in the kitchen preparing a special dinner for a birthday or homecoming, and if no one says "yuck" once, I'm thrilled. If anyone said, "Good meal, Mom," I'd require oxygen. One of my sons makes great chili, but you have to tell him so after each mouthful. If you miss once he says plaintively, "I know, I cooked the meat too long" or "Too much salt, right?"

A man who fixes a broken light plug will, for the next seven years, every time he turns on that lamp say, "Still working fine, huh!" If he digs a hole so that you can plant a shrub, he begins to act like he gave birth to it, making remarks like, "How's *my* azalea doing?" after you've been feeding and watering the blooming thing for years.

Besides needing encouragement, men are constitutionally unable to work around the house unassisted. However great their talents for plumbing repairs or wallpapering or just cleaning the bathroom, they require acolytes to fetch and hold, to bring coffee and Band-Aids. The only thing they don't want is advice.

Also, housework is a series of small details and men, bless them, are not so hot at little things. A male scientist may discover a moon around the planet Pluto, 2.8 billion miles from Earth, but he probably can't locate aspirins in the medicine chest. When it comes to his home, a man may know to the penny the assessed valuation and to the inch the square footage of the lot, but he doesn't know where the sugar is kept (even when it's a large jar marked s-u-g-a-r).

Then, too, most men are accustomed to rewards for their work. They are used to a pat on the back, letters of commendation and peer approval. So they find nothing but frustration doing a job that remains completely unnoticed until you stop doing it. One friend says she and her husband gave up assigning chores and content themselves with assigning blame.

This whole concept of role reversal has been very difficult for men, for they, like us, grew up with attitudes that now must change. They too require liberation and from more than just the sole financial burdens of the family. Men must be released from their stereotyped roles so that they can freely express *their* feelings. Men must be allowed to be afraid of mice, to hug their friends and kiss their fathers, to cry at movies and to do anything they think will make them look better and feel better about themselves. Why are we quick to ridicule a man for wearing a hairpiece or dyeing the hair he has? We admire a woman's wig and then say, "But did you catch the toup on that joker?" That's a stupid distinction.

Happily, as women have become more free, men in our society have had breakthroughs too. Men who never admitted they enjoyed cooking are now wearing aprons. They are becoming nurses, and terrific ones at that. And some are staying home with the kids while their wives go to work. But for the most part we still have a long way to go in breaking out of traditional roles.

The next generation will cope better with these changes. Today's middle-aged husband often has a hard time understanding his middle-aged wife. For one thing, men are not as flexible as women; they're slow to buy new ideas (and greeting cards). Nothing in their backgrounds has conditioned them to support their wives' ambitions. But they're trying because they love their wives and peace (not necessarily in that order). Just give them time; we can't expect miracles. As a saleslady once told me when I tried on a size-twelve dress, "This is Macy's, not Lourdes."

CHAPTER

FAMILIES ARE A STACKED DECK. OUR RELATIVES COME to us "as is" and we have no voice in choosing the parents or children, the aunts or uncles fate shuffles and deals out to us.

A husband is the only relation, the only "next of kin," a woman gets to select from among a varied assortment. Would that they were packaged like chocolates in a Whitman's Sampler with each goody clearly identified as to content of its interior—soft or hard, bitter or sweet. Nuts?

Nowadays at least women have greater options picking husbands and get more of a whack at sampling the merchandise. They are free, first and foremost, not to take a husband at all and can have sex and deep personal relationships with men without going into marriage vows and legalities. In years past only "loose women" dared to attempt such liaisons, and then found themselves outcasts. Most of our foremothers were delighted to be married, to have the security and social approval that accompanied the ring. When they fell in love (or hoped they had) marriage was the inevitable result. That is, if the loved one was suitable, for again, choices were more limited.

Until recently, marriage was seldom contemplated by people of different colors, faiths or nationalities. Interracial marriage was unheard of and often illegal. Interfaith marriages were ardently discouraged and nationality differences presented insurmountable barriers. Irish and Italians shared a common race and faith, but seldom intermarried.

Eyebrows were hoisted when a woman married a man who was shorter, younger or less educated than herself. One seldom married out of one's station in life, for class distinction was an issue. And unlike today, a woman also had to find a man who was not already married to another woman. How the old options narrowed!

In yesteryears, parents who strongly disapproved of a child's choice of spouse might throw a spanner in the works. And many parents disapproved. It has been well documented that behind every great man is an astonished mother-in-law. Today even parents with legitimate gripes are hard put to stop an offspring's misguided marriage. But still they try.

Aunt Margaret is very devout—what Aunt Adelaide called "a religious frantic." So when her daughter announced her intention to marry a twice-divorced ne'er-do-well, Aunt Margaret headed for Greymoor Monastery and returned laden with holy water and scapulars and a relic of one of the Saint Johns. And she settled down for some serious prayer. I asked if she was hoping her daughter would change her mind and she said no, the girl was too stubborn for that. She was praying for the fiancé. With a faith in the power of prayer so characteristic of the Irish, Aunt Margaret said, "I'm praying the bum drops dead."

It's hard to know what's best for your children, and ideally they should freely pick their own mates. But until recently that was difficult, not only because of the narrowness of choice available but also because courtship then did not encourage couples to know each other well before marriage. The segregation of men and women, the mystery of sexual differences, made friendships between them all but impossible.

I once heard a Catholic man regretting that his background had kept him from knowing women well as he grew up, because his moral training had made girls nothing more or less than an "occasion of sin." It was not only a sin to do something with Martha, but it was a sin to think about doing something with Martha, so he'd best avoid Martha altogether. When, later on, he married Martha, it was often difficult to reverse the pattern.

It was much the same in every religion, for fear and guilt about sex were the two great weapons parents had to keep their children from getting in trouble. And "getting into trouble" meant only one thing—pregnancy. For a girl it meant the ruination of her reputation and no decent man would have anything to do with her. For a boy it could mean a shotgun wedding and the end of all his dreams for the future.

That dynamic duo, fear and guilt, worked wonders, all things considered, but the result was that boys and girls didn't get to know each other as individuals, as people with specific needs. And vastly unsuited couples married each other, couples who wound up with nothing more in common than their last name. Like Steve and Butterfly McQueen.

Along with most mothers, I am ambivalent about

my grown children living with someone before marriage. There is the immorality (I know, I know, that middle-class mentality is showing), the lack of commitment and the potential for hurt and disappointment. But there is advantage in getting to know someone before taking the plunge, and especially before involving children, which counters some of the negative aspects. Too many of yesterday's marriages were miserable because the couple didn't have the foggiest notion of what they were getting into. Particularly if they married young, only to grow in different directions, or if they married for all the wrong reasons.

One cousin married just to get away from her parents and she knew less about her intended than Lois Lane knew about Clark Kent. My college roommate married a guy she'd never seen on a weekday. He seemed ever so charming (in old movies he was played by Peter Lawford), but under that thin veneer was another layer of thin veneer. She never suspected she was hitching up to a guy who if *boring* was an Olympic event would have more medals than Mark Spitz.

Only recently one old chum jumped into remarriage with a gentleman so wonderful that she couldn't understand how his first wife could have divorced him. She should have suspected something. He had an alarming number of redeeming features. By the time their second (month) anniversary came around she was shopping for a lawyer. Her new husband was, it seems, constantly clearing his throat with great coughs, bringing up huge amounts of phlegm which he then spit incredible distances. In all the time they'd dated he'd never once done that. We suggested this might be the reason he was so backed up. She, however, refused to be placated because she felt she'd also been deceived about his basic nature. Whereas in their courting days he had been an absolute rock, as a married man he greeted the smallest obstacle with hysteria. If he broke a shoelace or a cuff link rolled under the bed, off went his head and on went a windmill.

The point being that no one can know an intended spouse too well. A couple who sees each other only in dating situations often makes judgments that prove invalid. The quiet, brooding young man (Marlon Brando played him) who seemed to have such depth actually had nothing to say and a lousy disposition. Just as the cute little blonde (remember Sandra Dee?) who's so helpless and flustered can become a wife you hate to see raising your children or even ironing your shirts for that matter.

Having pontificated about how much consideration should be given to the selection of a husband, the values to be weighed and the qualities sought, I must now confess to appalling nonchalance in choosing my own. At a party one night the door opened, revealing the most magnificent-looking Marine lieutenant I'd ever seen, right off a recruiting poster (an accurate assumption, I later discovered). I said to my roommate, "See that guy in the doorway? I'm going to marry him." She laughed. I didn't. She said I must be crazy. Another accurate assumption.

He stood by the bar and the only way to get close was to keep going for drinks and I'd never before swallowed liquor, and when he finally noticed me, what he noticed was that I was blotto and needed some fresh air. Gallantly, he took me out for a walk. I repaid his kindness by throwing up on his shoes. A non-auspicious, if prophetic, beginning.

On our second date we decided to be married. To the great delight of my family. At twenty-three I was marked (down), an item that was not moving off the shelf and a year-end clearance sale had been considered. In fact, when Jack asked Dad if we could be married in six months—around Christmas—Dad shot back, "What the hell's the matter with Thanksgiving?" Given my parents' anxiety, that would have been uniquely suitable timing. Dad's sense of urgency, he delicately explained, came from his observation that, "She's looking at that guy like a starving man looks at a plate of spaghetti."

So, like almost everyone else, we married for all the wrong reasons. I thought he was too yummy to admire but not touch and he thought I was a good sport. But no body stays eternally yummy and one trip to the labor room cured me of being a good sport, and so, like everyone else, we had to adjust. To accept what we could not change and change what would not be accepted. To forgive (but never forget). And we've been terribly lucky—heavy on the lucky.

A marriage is like any successful partnership: the good things that come along are twice as good because there is someone to share them with. And the bad things are half the burden. Marriage can also create a situation where your combined strengths become greater than the sum of your individual strengths. This is a valid precept in marriage as it is in physics, where *synergism* describes a total effect greater than the sum of two effects taken separately. It works for chemical elements and it worked for Rodgers and Hammerstein, Amos and Andy, Mutt and Jeff, Evans and Novak. A good collaboration can often outdistance two individual efforts and God knew that when He (or She) made babies the result of combined endeavor. Children are ideally raised by two parents, one of each. There have been many wonderful families raised by single parents, but most of those parents would tell you it was doing things the hard way. And Jimmy the Greek didn't get rich betting against the odds.

There are those endeavors where individual effort is sufficient and the loner can achieve. Running, channel swimming, writing, painting are all suitable to the single person. But it takes two to Ping-Pong, two to fight or play gin rummy or create life.

For any woman who would be a housewife, a man in the form of a husband is essential. But when she determines to be a mother, the need becomes pressing. Men historically make the best fathers (also the worst). Their initial investment, however, in "Project: Baby" is one of purely carnal pleasure while a woman gets to be pregnant for nine months afterward, which tends to dim the glow of the original encounter. And no one, I mean no one, in the maternity ward exhibits the vaguest interest in *The Joy of Sex.*

Once baby comes home the father's role firms up and in the best of worlds he learns to care for and enjoy his new little tax deduction. One of the most positive aspects of the new awareness of sexual roles is the participation of the father in raising his children.

Ever since the Industrial Revolution took men away

from their homes and lands to work, fathers have been too often peripheral figures—nothing more than weary men arriving home each evening to have supper and dispense justice. Breathes there a child who wasn't threatened with, "Wait till your father gets home"? How proper, then, that men are beginning to take more positive roles in their children's lives than merely breadwinner and avenging angel. Too long have they been forced into positions over which they have small control. Because to support their families, fathers have to be away from them so much that often they find themselves virtual outsiders.

In a lovely old book on homemaking published in 1898, the lady author notes, "There are American fathers richer and poorer who suffer from absolute loneliness as the years creep on, who seem to their families in reality very little beyond purse holders. The good man of the house has a right to be treated with loving consideration by wife and children. Although occasionally he may repeat in their hearing a twice-told tale or expect them to laugh at a jest which is somewhat worn, it is small credit to young people to be polite and patient and even deferential to their father."

So Daddy-the-Dunce did not begin with Dagwood. And neither did keeping Daddy in the dark. Most wives are guilty of keeping things from their husbands —things they have every right to know. We do it without malice. Intending to be kind or keep peace, plumbers' bills get tucked away, price tags are cut off, drapes are pulled to cover a broken window and report cards are hidden.

And if every father occasionally feels like an outsider, every mother finds herself in the middle. When father confronts child (or child confronts father) mother has eternally been the unindicted coconspirator. None of us like it, but we accept that "it goes with the territory." And, like everything else, eventually we get good at it.

I've had my moments, as Mama had hers, but Grandma was the best (or worst depending on your viewpoint). She not only made famous the line, "It's not a fit night out for man nor beast—let your father go," but she saw to it that Grandpa went to his grave never knowing his son Frankie spent five years in high school. Once or twice he asked, "Shouldn't that boy be graduating soon?" and Grandma would reply, quite impatiently, "Glory be to God, didn't he just start?"

Volumes have been written about women being repressed by motherhood, but let us here note that fatherhood was seldom peaches and champagne either. Mama may have been tied to her house and babies, but my father was hardly "doing his thing" scampering back and forth behind the counter of his West Side diner fourteen hours a day. My mother-in-law may have had it rough with five children in ten years, but her husband wasn't fulfilling himself hauling freight off Pier 9 in Jersey City.

The two-martini lunch and interoffice hanky-panky may be *de rigueur* in some circles, but the men I see— the policemen and washer repairmen, the mailmen and butchers—are the ordinary men, straining and pulling to make enough money to care for their families. They're ordinary men who, however weary, lie awake nights staring at the ceiling, worrying about bills which come in faster than the money; worrying about having enough insurance to care for their families if the work and worry should kill them too soon.

There have always been men who were bounders, who drank away the grocery money or spent it on floozies, and our family had its share. And their wives put up with them, God knows why. One relative had a husband who was a lying-in-the-gutter drunk, but she couldn't leave him, "Because he never looks at another woman." He never looked at her either, but that didn't seem to count.

Mostly though, I grew up watching good fathers sacrificing for their children and all too often never getting to know or enjoy them. The new emphasis on Daddy's participation is a welcome change in family life.

There used to be an apocryphal story (which rang all too true) about a mother breaking the news to her children that their dog had been killed by a car while they were at school. She told them softly that Laddie died and was prepared to offer some comforting details about heaven and death as the end of pain. But the children were so calm, thanked her for telling them and ran out to play. They began calling, "Laddie, Laddie," and the bewildered mother went out to tell them they must understand that he'd never answer their call again. Laddie was dead. The children began to sob uncontrollably, explaining, "But we thought you said Daddy."

CHAPTER

9

SOMETIME IN THE FUTURE, CURRENT MEANS OF CONception and childbirth may be obsolete and you won't need nuptials or even sex to reproduce. You'll just run your sunburn peelings down to the corner druggist and have him whip up a clone. Or better still, you could lurk about the pool at the Beverly Hills Hotel and try to snag some of Candice Bergen's peelings. A duplicate person might be ordered in any size and you could specify straight teeth and classic nose, good reflexes and metabolism. The world could become glutted with perfect people.

The implications are infinite. Lane Bryant would go into chapter eleven. Jack La Lanne would finally be a has-been. Plastic surgeons would have to scramble for accident victims, running elbow to elbow with ambulance-chasing lawyers. Orthodontists would be convening at the unemployment office. And if some couple carelessly produced a child who looked like Ernest Borgnine, he could be a bigger rage than Burt Reynolds, pursued as an erotic image by *Playgirl* for their centerfold.

But for now, we who would have children are stuck

with sex and marriage. And when you give it hard thought, the wonder is not that many marriages break apart, but that so many succeed against the long-shot odds. For not only is marriage entered into for specious reasons, but it is the most inherently unworkable relationship. It involves living with someone about whom you know the worst and also with someone who seldom sees you at your best. In an Irish play there is a line about marriage combining the maximum loneliness with the minimum privacy, but that seems an unduly dour, if typically Gaelic view.

In addition, we marry for love and we're told that love is giving, "love is never having to say you're sorry," or even, love is never having to ask how much? The fact is, love is a contact sport that can be jolly good fun, but may bruise or cut or break your heart. And there's a lot of rubbing the wrong way—the ultimate act of love requires friction. It was ever thus.

We are assured that it's harder to keep marriage going with today's pressures and conflicts. But perhaps the difference is no more or less than the full-speed-ahead mentality of our times. If our grandparents lived day by day, and our parents lived minute by minute, we seem to live second by second. Fittingly, in the age of the second.

Today quite average folk talk about a second car, a second home, a second wife, a second husband, a second family; most of which require a second job. We're after a second chance and some yearn to be "born again." The catch is that we're caught in a world where no one gets out alive, and lifetimes come one to a customer. No replays. No do-overs. We can neither rewrite our past nor draft our future. But having been made aware of the possibilities, we know we want it all.

Is this, perchance, why we expect so much of marriage? In simpler times a husband was expected to make the money to pay his family's bills. He was not expected to be a plumber, painter, carpenter, mechanic and Little League coach. Nor was he expected to keep all his hair, a flat stomach and be an accomplished sexual athlete.

A wife was expected to care for a home and children. She was not expected to be a combination Jeeves, Tonto and the Happy Hooker: "Tennis clothes are laid out, m'Lord"; "Great serve, Kemo Sabay"; "Too tired to make whoopee, Big Boy?"

It is bandied about that sex is the problem with marriage; that monogamy is monotonous and each of us requires variety. But realistically, not only is the basic apparatus rather standard but, as Woody Allen so poetically put it, "Of the fifty-six possible positions for sex, only eight can be achieved without laughing." Which goes along with the line attributed to an actress's fifth bridegroom: "I know what's expected of me; I just don't know how to make it interesting."

The Great Lover flitting from flower to flower has always seemed an invalid image. The Great Lover should be one who can satisfy the same partner for years—*that* takes talent and imagination, patience and persistence. And a strong back.

Recent books written by women totally preoccupied with sex make one marvel. Don't they have mothers to call? Closets to clean? Bills to pay? A living to make?

Undies to Woolite? Just what are they trying to prove? That women can write dirtier than men?

Or have I missed the point again? (My children feel there is a spot for me in the *Guinness Book of World Records* under *"Most Points Missed."*) Is sex after all the bread of life while I've been treating it like the butter—seeing it add immeasurably to the flavor of the dish but hardly a satisfying meal in itself? The problem is perhaps that I was brought up on movies where sexy was Cary Grant taking Deborah Kerr's hand and leading her up the stairs. *That* was sexy. Everything else was left to the imagination—which could exclude unbuttoning shirts, tugging off stockings (they don't call them No-Nonsense panty hose for nothing), unlacing shoes and all the other ticky-tacky necessities of a sexual encounter.

This generation, however, has been brought up on movies that feature the ticky-tacky. There are slurping kisses as erotic as guppies in a tank and full frontal nudity, although the unhappy truth is that almost everyone over twenty looks better in clothes. Nothing is left to fancy on screens where I've seen Jane Fonda pee and Anthony Quinn's backside.

Between explicit movies and the sex manuals which reduce lovemaking to something only slightly more romantic than touch-typing, sex is on its way to becoming so boring no one will want to be bothered. Creating a strong world market for those nifty clones.

The problems with marriage, unfortunately, go beyond sex and boredom, and the reality is that many marriages are unhappy. Is this, however, a reflection on marriage or might it not be just because so many people are unhappy? Some people are born crying, live complaining and die disappointed. They slowly chew each bitter pill instead of swallowing it whole, watering it down with a little patience and humor. And these unhappy individuals don't make happy marriages. For where one has a right to rely on a spouse for affection and consideration, no one can expect anyone else to make him happy.

A friend once stopped by our house on his way from the "best wedding" he'd ever been to, because two stinkers married each other. So not only would they be inflicting misery on someone who richly deserved it but two decent people had been spared a lifetime of grief.

I'd never quite thought of it that way, but it can be heartwarming to see people marry who, for better or worse, deserve each other. And belong together. Like Uncle Dan and Aunt Aggie. He had a big paunch and she had a huge bosom and when they danced they fit together like pieces in a jigsaw puzzle. Grandma claimed, "God made them and matched them." Sad to say, not all matches are made by a benevolent deity.

Each fall a local ski club has a day when you can swap your outgrown equipment for someone else's gear that is more suitable. Wouldn't it be lovely if that could be done with couples? Get them all together one afternoon for some good clean swaps. A wife who loves keeping house could swap her gadabout husband for a man who loves to putter about the yard and appreciates a good cook. The lady who must be on the go could swap her housebound husband for the first wife's gadabout. Neatniks could pair with neatniks, boozers with boozers, screamers would at last have someone screaming back and those with love to give might find appreciative takers. And maybe even be loved in return. So much unhappiness could be avoided. But it's never going to be that easy. A tight husband is dramatically harder to ditch than a tight ski boot.

When I was growing up, divorce was something that happened in Hollywood. Now it's standard procedure everywhere; a part of our core mentality which prefers replacement to repair. Party conversation no longer centers around "What's up," but "Who's whose." And you are obligated to hear sleazy details about the reasons for the divorce and they almost all boil down to that old chestnut about greener grass. The career girl covets the security of home and family afforded the housewife and the housewife thinks a career is glamorous and exciting.

We had a neighbor who decided that she'd missed something by not having a proper career and that she needed more self-expression. Her husband was a real peach about it. He paid her university tuition so that she could study social work. He hired a live-in maid to relieve her of household duties and took on extra work to pay for it all. But when she came home from school, she talked to the maid about racial oppression and to her daughter about consciousness raising and never had a minute for her husband. So by the time she had a master's, he had a mistress, and now his ex-wife is expressing the hell out of herself, running about giving good causes a bad name. And devoting her energies to counseling women about what rotters men are.

The greener-grass syndrome strikes men as well. Those with families begrudge the freedom of bachelor friends while those same bachelors may think they'd find contentment if they had a loving family to make life worthwhile.

Not only can someone else's life-style seem more appealing, but someone else's spouse often looks like a better deal than yours. Someone else's husband is just never seen picking his teeth with a matchbook cover. He listens when you speak and doesn't needle you about your family. And many a man leaves his wife for the "other woman," an affectionate, adoring, beautifully groomed young lady who never nags him to call his mother or put up the screens. And who doesn't own a flannel nightgown or a nasal inhaler. Yet.

A Marine Corps buddy of Jack's had a wife, children, house, mortgage, dog and cat—the whole catastrophe. Mr. Suburbia. In his mid-forties he ran off with a young girl, a free spirit with a motorcycle and a pad in Soho. Given the generation gap, we were hard put to imagine what they talked about since she thought The Ink Spots were something you take to the cleaners and he thought Elton John was a kind of bathroom fixture; he thought biorhythms was a new dance step and she thought the lindy hop was a plane trip to Paris. But he became a swinger, let his hair (what there was of it) grow longer and got himself some bulky jewelry, including a bunch of rings that made his old Italian father fear he'd joined the mob and was sporting brass knuckles.

Le Swinger hadn't been married to Toot-Toot-Tootsie for a month when he was informed that they really needed a decent car and that an apartment with a doorman would be safer. And that she'd grown bored with jeans and opened a charge account at Bloomingdale's. So his new life-style has become his old life-style plus an alimony check. And last year, at forty-nine, he became a daddy again, noting wistfully that, "When the kid graduates from college I'll be seventy. If he's smart."

Our family has not managed to avoid divorce, although it's still the exception. The most recent one involved dear Aunt Adelaide's youngest daughter who was married to an authentic creep—Quasimodo in a leisure suit. When he walked out on his family, Aunt Adelaide summed up her emotions in two words, "Little loss." Besides, she told us, he was *important*, you know, can't have sex." Come to find out he was involved with his young secretary and was far from "important." He just gave at the office.

CHAPTER

CONSUMER ADVOCATES GET A LOT OF MILEAGE OUT of *caveat emptor*, let the buyer beware. It's also a swell idea for you who would trade one spouse for another because, as with all secondhand merchandise, very few people let go of a really good thing. If her first husband was a carouser and barfly, there might be a reason he resisted coming home. If his first wife looks ten years older than he, be aware that nothing so ages a woman as marriage to a dull man. A used spouse is sometimes every bit as reliable as a used car. Aunt Molly used to claim, "There are few real bargains" (a philosophy that kept her contented to remain single for life).

Perhaps what is needed is a consumers' guide to selecting a spouse. There is no literature on how to choose your mate, although there is a plethora of books dealing with the problems your marriage may engender. Our village library has four shelves of books on marriage and not one of them tells you the things you really must know.

They don't tell you that the wife gets the lion's share of the closet space while the husband gets the

119

bottom shelf of the medicine cabinet. They fail to mention that you don't prove you love your wife by bringing home posies but by taking out the garbage; and you don't prove you love a man by going to bed with him but by getting up with him.

What these experts don't know about marital fights could fill four more shelves. They tell you quaint rules like, "Don't ever go to bed angry." That doesn't work at all. You force yourself to contrive a reconciliation with that insensitive oaf/cow just because it's bedtime and you'll lie awake all night, gnawed at by repressed rage and plotting revenge. Whereas when you go to bed furious you are lulled to sleep by the certain knowledge that your warming self-pity is justified inasmuch as you are truly the most undervalued wife/unappreciated husband. You'll sleep like a rock.

These experts tell you all the goody-two-shoes rules and never make mention of the well-established "Rubrics of Marital Fighting." So we're all forced to learn them through trial and error, wasting valuable time. Actually these definitive regulations are quite elementary if you just keep in mind that all other rules of conduct between adversaries are simply reversed.

Unlike those guidelines established by the Marquess of Queensberry, in marital fights you must always try to hit below the belt. Unlike legal disputes, there is no statute of limitations—no previous infraction is too far back in time to be dredged up and rehashed. Unlike the Geneva conventions, there is no safe zone marked by a red cross—marital fights are no-holds-barred, go-for-the-jugular brawls. But not free-for-alls. No, indeed; they are as stylized as a Kabuki dance. And all these battles end in a draw. There is no recorded instance where a husband or wife was declared the winner (or admitted to being the loser).

Marital wars are, however, fought along much the same lines as all traditional warfare. The initial skirmish may be different each time (although not necessarily, or even usually), but once the battle lines are drawn the war is fought with conventional weapons and predictable tactics until both parties can't remember how it started.

At this point peace overtures are commenced and these are ritualistic and couched in the interrogative: "Can I get you a drink?" "Did you notice I pressed your suit?" Or just simply, "How about it, honey?" And it is at this stage that treaties are consummated, and we who have been there can testify that some of the great moments in marriage involve consummating treaties.

Happily, domestic fights do not require SALT talks because there are no newly perfected strategic arms to cope with as battles are eternally fought with the same weapons. The weapons are words, which can be flung out or aimed softly, depending on the combat conditions. The only inhumane weapon that should be outlawed by international convention is silence. Silence is very effective but inordinately cruel. Words wound but silence tears you apart.

These fights, distasteful as they are, will go ever so much more smoothly once you know the rules. And more quickly too, because after enough practice most couples are able to dispense with the preliminary sparring and proceed promptly to the main event. Each partner will eventually hone the whole discourse down to just that one phrase or word guaranteed to set the other one off. Like the old Groucho show, you learn to, "Say the magic word and see the duck fly off the handle."

In this regard it is helpful to remember that there are certain key phrases guaranteed to move the fight along to a swifter if more heated climax. The majority of these phrases are androgynous and can be used by either partner with equal effectiveness, although "nag" is customarily applied to the female and "needle" to the male. But most are unisex accusatory phrases that begin, "You never . . ."; "You always . . ."; "Your mother . . ."; "Your precious job. . . ." (Formerly zapped almost exclusively at the male, the latter is lately proving quite effective against the female as well.)

There is, "Money. That's all you care about." "That kid gets more like you every day." And the old standby, "Once, just once, can't you admit *you're* wrong?" These phrases of course just skim the surface in the possible litany of marital accusations. Perhaps someday the Ford Foundation will award a grant to some graduate student with a tape recorder who could catalog the prime areas of marital discord, reducing them down to numbers. And we could all save a lot of time by simply shouting, "Numbers two, seven, eleven, fifteen and forty-three, you big jerk."

And in case you still think your marriage is an original, your problems peculiar to our times, look at this admonition to women from that same 1898 book.

Remember that you are married to a man who

may sometimes be mistaken; be prepared for im-perfections.

Every so often let your husband have the last word; it will gratify him and be of no particular loss to you.

Let him know more than you do once in a while; it keeps up his self respect and you are none the worse for admitting that you are not actually infallible.

I also had very good advice from Aunt Blanche, who urged me to give and take and then give again, and to always think of what I was saying. She told about putting away her winter clothes, but some of her best things had to be dry-cleaned first. Her husband, trying to help, insisted on doing the errands one Saturday, taking her things to the cleaner and a bunch of old clothes to the Goodwill bin. You can guess the rest. A week later when she went to the cleaners, there were all the Goodwill things hanging neatly inside plastic baggies. And she never told her husband. Even when he groused about her buying a new winter coat the next year, she never told him, because he would have felt terrible and nothing could be gained.

Now plays have been written and songs sung about great love. Lovers who sacrificed their lives for love or abandoned thrones for love. And given the right timing, I think most of us are capable of such gestures, extraordinary though they might appear. But to not tell your husband he tossed your best clothes into the Goodwill bin—very few of us are capable of such devotion (or self-control).

My aunt's point was that while you always hear how good and warming and necessary it is to say loving words to your spouse, usually more love can be shown by keeping your mouth shut. By not saying, "I told you not to buy that stock," or "I knew your brother would never pay back the loan," or "Second helpings; that's some diet you're on," or the ever-popular, "You've already had two beers."

We all have our faults and seldom enjoy being reminded of them. Marriage encounter encourages that you tell each other the things bothering you so that they can be resolved. My mother-in-law who's been married over fifty years said, "That's nonsense. I told him his faults all the time and he told me mine and we certainly never paid any attention to each other."

The comforting thing is that if you can stick it out, after enough years of marriage, your vices and virtues interchange. The tardy partner becomes prompt and "vicer" versa. Faults become less glaring. Or some of them do. My poor husband is still living in hope. He claims to have no fear that any success I might have writing a book will change me because I've always been an insufferable know-it-all.

And that's true enough, although it's not totally my fault. I happened to be born with a rare brain damage that prevents me from remembering where I put the tax returns but permits me to name all of Mickey Rooney's wives. The more trivial the subject, the more total my recall. This cerebral malfunction also compels me to have an opinion on everything, the strength of my conviction being in adverse proportion to my familiarity with the subject. In other words, the less I know the more positive I am. But after all these years, Jack has learned to compensate by adjusting his perceptions accordingly. In other words, he tunes me out. I often don't pay attention to him, and there are things we don't tell each other. And all the books would assure you such a relationship is doomed. And we might yet split up, although if I were a betting person I'd lay odds that we'd kill each other first.

There are all kinds of marriages and lucky for me the most unlikely ones often work best. Couples whose futures seem less bright than Nicholas and Alexandra's muddle through while couples divorce who appear more made for each other than Ken and Barbie. If there is such a thing as a perfect marriage I've never seen it, but there are good, strong marriages possible to those who would keep some sense of humor and perspective. My own parents had a typical workable marriage—it went forward and slid back, went up and down, and they could fight like Kilkenny cats. But when things were calm again, Mama would voice the feeling every woman ever married to a man has known. She'd smile at Dad across the room and say softly, "I'm just so glad I didn't murder him yesterday."

CHAPTER

As a little girl in Brooklyn in the late 1930s, for nine cents I could go to a Saturday movie matinee at the Kent on Coney Island Avenue. Along with two features there were several shorts and one serial, continued next week. The serials were invariably Westerns where Indians were the villains. You remember the kind, the wagon train was seen from a great distance below in the valley and then in the near foreground appeared a FEATHER. Said feather was attached to the head of a fierce-looking savage who ultimately attacked those innocents in the wagon train.

Another variation showed a woman working around her ranch house, usually fetching water, while children played at her feet and the same feather cropped up. Her husband was always off somewhere, so she'd gather in the kiddies, grab the family rifle from above the fireplace and start shooting out the window like Annie Oakley at her zenith. That was the serial that scared me most because I could identify with that woman, that mother, having to be so constantly on the alert lest her children be nailed by Indian arrows.

She had the life of Riley compared to today's aver-

129

age mother, who has more sneaky villains to cope with. She is birthing babies who can get cancer from her breast milk, bringing up children who can be brain damaged by their cereals or given tumors by their pajamas. The water coming out of her kitchen tap may make them sterile and she sends them out to play in "industrial fallout" and breathe air of "unacceptable quality." About the only thing an American mother doesn't have to worry about today is rampaging savages.

Mothers also have rougher going now because they are constantly being told what they're doing wrong. They find themselves accused of using the wrong psychology, the wrong approach and the wrong peanut butter. And as if that isn't enough, if they choose to pass up the rewards of an outside job, they find themselves criticized for being "underpotentialized."

We have friends who are very into reincarnation and I've given the idea some thought. But when I see our world so full of contradictions, ironies and frustrations, I often wonder if this life, here and now, is actually the afterlife and is the hell we earned by misbehaving earlier.

Just when medical advances have given mothers good assurance that their babies would be able to live healthy lives, it is proposed that having babies can be dangerous to their self-esteem. Children are seen as stumbling blocks on the road to fulfillment and flies in the ointment of self-expression.

The women's movement first pointed a guilty finger at men as our oppressors, but recently children have been perceived as negative forces. Are we being urged to show our outrage toward men by neglecting their children? Probably not, but the rationale behind the unpopularity of child care is tough to fathom.

Aunt Jo had been baby-sitting for her two young grandsons and they had all but wrecked her house. By the time their mother picked them up, Jo was limp with exhaustion and said, "I'd just like to tell all these young mothers who leave their little children and go off to a job that they're nothing but spineless cowards."

In rearing young children, there are times when going to work as a piano mover or steel-furnace stoker does appear to be taking the easy way out. And when a woman has been trained for lucrative work it may seem a waste of time to stay home with a baby. Especially so when society appears to view child care as dull and unstimulating.

The truth is that not only can raising a child be more challenging than capturing a great white shark, it can be very rewarding. Had I sculpted my five children out of marble, I might be hailed as a genius. But having given birth to them, fed and nurtured and shaped them into sensitive living people, my life's work is considered by many a meaningless waste.

When we were expecting our first baby, both families were thrilled and we were just so proud of ourselves. My dad, always the voice of reason, burst our bubble with the brutal truth: "It didn't take brains." Any female properly equipped and given male cooperation can bear a child. Raising him, however, is not for the faint of heart. It requires courage and fortitude. But there is a joy that comes with watching your child develop which truly feeds the spirit. And if that is not fulfilling, I can't envision what is.

Edward Steichen took a famous photograph of a poor black woman, thin and drawn, wearing a shabby sweater, an old kerchief around her head. On either side of her cling two young children and the title underneath is from Proverbs 3:18. "She is a tree of life to them."

A mother, however plain or ordinary, is the most important person in a child's life. What she gives or does not give him affects him eternally. A baby is completely dependent. It will take years before he can minimally care for himself. And for a mother, filling his needs gives no small satisfaction, no small sense of importance.

Too much emphasis has been placed on the negative side of having babies. You hear how confining it is, that you'll be tied up and slowed down, but no one ever tells you that giving birth is embarking on a life-long love affair. And like all love affairs, it's pretty physical in the beginning.

Babies need better P.R., and perhaps the way to drum up renewed interest in having them would be to put out a book on the "sensual mother." And I mean sensual in its purest sense. Because nothing prepares you for the delight you'll experience handling that tiny body.

Babies are sloppy creatures, which may be why bathing them is such pleasure. You not only get all the nooks and crannies flushed out and smelling sweet, but you get to run your hands over those little arms and legs, over the soft, round belly and the behind that could fit in a teacup. And stroking this skin is a tactile extravaganza; it's softer than a kitten's ear.

Like snowmen, babies have no proper necks, but there is a place right behind the ears and down an inch where head meets torso that is heaven to nuzzle. Babies have delicate hands and lie with palms opened, and you'd be astounded how much time a grown woman can waste watching her infant rearrange his fingers. Babies also have exquisite feet, especially compared to the ones you're used to seeing—those bunioned, corned, hammertoed jobs sticking out of your friends' summer sandals. And when you turn their feet over, the undersides of the toes resemble nothing more than tiny, perfectly graduated pink beads.

Babies' heads, with or without fuzzy hair, are wondrous. Miraculously, the tops smell sweet no matter what nasty business is going on below and on either side there are ears like moon shells. They have eyes like tiddledywinks and noses so tiny you wonder they can breathe through them. And mouths shaped like lifesavers and they smile a lot; smiles that may or may not be gas but are sweet, and innocent smiles like porpoises.

Contrary to myth, babies are not inveterate screamers. Mama assured me that they only howl for a reason and you must never ignore a crying baby, which provided all the excuse I needed to hold mine. So maybe my left shoulder smelled perpetually like spoiled Camembert. And if my left hip took on a shelflike contour after years of being straddled by toddlers, my right hip is no great shakes either.

Once while I was doing volunteer work in an institution housing disturbed youngsters, the staff psychologist lectured on research in dealing with hysterical children. He said studies proved medication took too long to work and slapping them only added to their hostility. So it had been concluded that the indicated method of dealing with a hysterical child was to hold him tightly against your body until his sobbing subsided. How come mothers always knew that?

Physical contact is as important and as reassuring to a child as it is to any animal. Like puppies or chicks huddled together against their mothers and each other, babies instinctively turn toward you to snuggle. They love to be held, especially propped against the left shoulder where they can feel your heartbeat, a comforting thump they've gotten used to in your womb.

Now if babies are a sensual experience, toddlers are pure challenge. They get into your cupboards and under your skin and just when you're convinced you should have opted for the convent after all, they'll come toward you with a bunch of dandelions clutched in a grubby hand and all is forgiven.

But then there's toilet training. When a mother tells you there's nothing to it and her child had it down pat by thirteen months, one thing is certain. She is lying. I had slow learners, I'll grant you that, but most mothers who aren't lugging a diaper bag to kindergarten registration are lucky. My boys encouraged one another. One would sit on the john straining away and the other would kneel beside him yelling, "Keep on going, it's still one piece." It's yucky, but better than my kid brother who used to pluck his out of his diapers and fling it across the room. One of my uncles, home on leave in 1943, had to share a bedroom with him and announced that thereafter enemy flack would be meaningless.

Even toddlers have their sensual good points. They have soft, downy fuzz on back and limbs which almost compensates for their skin getting more firm to the touch. And they are very affectionate, inclined to jump into your lap almost every time you make one. Toddlers are huggers, given to planting sloppy kisses. They are most appealing, however, like Botticelli angels, when sleeping. Which may be what people mean when they say it's not the quantity of time you're with your children but the quality—that most of the time you're with them they're asleep.

When they get older the sensual delights diminish, and the physical strain becomes less heroic as they become capable of independent activity. At this point a new dimension is added. Drama. Anyone who finds caring for children ho-hum clearly never heard a little boy's voice calling from upstairs, "My parrakeet is missing and the cat is covered with feathers." Or that great old showstopper, "Has anyone seen my snake?" They never experienced the frozen horror of seeing their four-year-old walk past the attic window. Or the shock of learning that the ten cents he just swallowed was two nickels.

Raising children taxes not only your nerves but your ingenuity. It isn't easy outsmarting little kids, at least it never was for me, but it can be done. If they insist on more of a selection at lunchtime, you can say, "O.K. Do you want your jelly sandwich now or in five minutes?" or, "Would you like your jelly sandwich whole or cut in half?" But you never, never, offer a choice of sandwich (or anything else) unless you have lost all regard for your sanity.

It helps to be positive, for indecision on your part is perceived as a sign of weakness, leaving you open to further attack. For instance, in answer to the question, "When are we leaving for the park?" you never answer, "Soon," or, "In a little while." With great authority you say, "Ten ninety-six A.M. and don't ask me that again." By the time your child (or your teen-ager for that matter) figures that out you're ready already.

Another rule about children is that you never, ever, put ideas in their heads. At one Thanksgiving dinner a maiden aunt narrowly escaped being strangled by me after telling the small children, "Now whatever you do, don't put peas up your nose."

The one and only good thing most people believe about raising children is, I'm loathe to admit, a lie. Being around children does not keep you young. Quite the contrary. As they slice their skins and crack their bones and get lost on crowded beaches a mother's face becomes a topographic map of worry wrinkles and frown lines. I informed my three eldest boys that when I'm fifty they should all be out working and they owe me reparations in the form of plastic surgery. They said not to count on it, that in another five years Arnold Schwarzenegger couldn't lift my face.

CHAPTER

———————————

12

GRANDMA HAD SEVEN CHILDREN AND NO THEORIES about raising them. My next-door neighbor has one child and seventy theories. Mama practiced only one, known loosely as "judicious neglect," which fostered freedom if not license. And she pressed self-sufficiency on us with a line my children have learned to loathe. Every plea of, "But I don't know how to (make a sandwich, polish silver, iron a shirt . . .)" was met with, "You'll never learn any younger."

More than theories, what a mother needs is flexibility. As the kids say, "You gotta be able to go to your left." Children pass through stages and your best bet is to roll with the punches. Each stage has its problems and its compensations, and ironies abound. You spend years urging them to bathe once a day, followed by years of begging them to bathe *only* once a day. You urge them to think about their appearance and go bonkers when all they ever seem to think about is their appearance.

As toddlers they may have pleaded to be held in your arms, but adolescents hate having to talk to you in public so forget about holding a hand. And don't even think about touching the hair. If you find yourself longing for some physical contact, there are devious ruses that can be implemented. You can pretend to have taken up palmistry as an excuse to hold a hand. You can say he looks feverish as an excuse to put your lips on his forehead. Or you can do what I did when I saw my children lunging toward adolescence and beginning to squirm away from me. Have another baby.

The hardest part was telling the children—not knowing how they'd react. So I fixed a special dinner and their father told them he had an announcement to make. We were going to have a baby. They were all smiles. "A baby what?" Slowly they realized it was to be a baby person. Smiles dimmed. Actually it was supposed to be a baby girl called Amy, since with three boys and one girl I knew the Lord must be anxious to balance things out.

By the time Tommy was born, however, the children all rather liked the idea and when we brought him home from the hospital they fought over holding him. I'd wanted this baby to nuzzle and squeeze and found myself waiting on line. By the time he was a toddler there was some concern that, like the feet of some church statues are worn down by the stroking of the faithful, his small head would flatten out from persistent patting and kissing.

He's nine now and his head is none the worse for wear, and having him probably kept us all sane through the teen-age years of the other children. Teen-agers never bore you. But they do everything else. They madden you, frighten you, humiliate you, amuse you, worry you, help you. They devour enormous amounts of food and create bushels of laundry. They bend your rules and wrinkle your car.

You know they've had too many beers the night you call downstairs to see who's there and the answer is, "Nobody. Go back to bed." You know they're in love when they begin to look like the cat when he ate the parrakeet. And you bite your tongue when the girl they bring home for dinner looks like Tiny Tim but not that feminine.

The older they get the more complicated they are. And just as they finally become people whom you can converse with and who can help paint the house, they also become people who are never around. Then one September day you find yourself at a college campus depositing your child into a world you will never be part of (except lucky you gets to pick up the tab).

Having trained your children to be independent and self-sufficient, you may be surprised to find how devastated you are when they turn out to be independent and self-sufficient. Each time we've dropped a new freshman at a college dorm I've thought that there should be something you could take to get you through the experience. Eighteen years ago when that baby was wrenched from your body, you were given a whiff of gas. But painless separation from your grown child has not yet been perfected, unless you're lucky (or unlucky) enough to have a kid who's such a creep you're relieved to be rid of him.

There are probably parents who honestly can't wait until their children are out of the house, but I don't know any. I don't even know any teen-agers who are creeps. They can be thoughtless and self-centered, but are usually without malice or pretext. And they are funny and they are vulnerable, caught between child and adult and never sure which direction to go.

When our oldest was just eighteen, he headed into the city Easter night to his first rock concert, and it was his big moment. But even so, going out the door he said, "It's gonna be great, but I kinda hate to miss *The Wizard of Oz.*"

Teen-agers have an unfortunate image they don't deserve. Those who don't know them complain that they are boisterous and addicted to awful music. Those who know them have the same complaint, but we also know they are children who need more love and attention than they'd want you to realize. However, even we who love them often complain about our own and knock them and make cracks about them. Maybe we do that because so few of us really know how to express our love, how to go about giving praise or even how to handle a compliment.

When a friend tells you your son helped her with bundles at the market and was so polite, too often you say, "Sure. Outside of the house he's polite. You should catch him at home." If you're told your daughter looked lovely in her prom gown, your predictable reply is, "She always looks good when she's out. But you should see her room—what a slob."

We have friends who created with their own hands the most charming home out of a rundown old farmhouse and every time someone told them how lovely it was, their standard reply was, "But it doesn't have a basement." Tell a man how terrific his wife looks and he'll say, "She should. Do you have any idea how much that outfit cost?" Tell her and she says, "This old thing?"

It may all be tied up with a heritage of denied feelings. As a child you'd say, "I'm hungry," and some adult would shoot back, "No, you're not. You just ate." You'd say, "I hate Freddie," and be told, "You don't hate Freddie. He's your brother." It was supposed to give you character, it didn't always work. Instead it often made you unsure of yourself, mistrusting of your perceptions, and you went into the cold world uninsulated by self-esteem and confidence. And so you allowed other people to tell you how to feel and what to want.

When you don't trust your own instincts it's easy to be taken in by experts and authorities. But the truth is, very few people are as smart as you believe they are, including yourself, and you are probably smarter than you think. It's a mistake to put such faith in experts that you don't question, especially when dealing with doctors and teachers and child psychologists. They may all be proficient in their fields, but no one knows your child better than you do. When it comes to our children, love is not so blind. A little nearsighted perhaps, but not blind. And nature has provided parents with terrific instincts if they'd just trust them.

Too many experts are telling mothers what to think and how to behave, and we want so much to do right by our children that we take all this advice like something chiseled in stone and delivered from a mountaintop. But the fact of our own existence testifies to our ancestors' ability to raise children without books or psychologists. They're not all bad and may even give a helpful hint, but experts don't have all the answers and if you want proof go talk to their children.

It goes back to "common sense isn't so common." If it were, we would all realize that children become what they imitate. Treated kindly, they'll probably become kind adults, but met with indifference they can turn into indifferent adults. They won't become trustworthy until they've learned they can trust you and they'll never learn to give love unless you show them how. And it's fairly predictable that the less attention a small child receives the more he'll require as an adult.

The saying goes, "Kids are people too." When your friend leaves an umbrella behind, you call after her, "You forgot something." But when your child leaves behind his lunch box, too often he's hit with, "I'd like to live to see the day that you'd walk out of this house without forgetting your head if it wasn't attached to your shoulders." Most of us mothers, however obtuse, learn that our children treat others as we treat them. I got the message the first time I saw my three-year-old, hands on hips, yelling at his little brother, "You're giving me a nervous breakdown."

With children, as with marriage, you can go far with a little patience and humor. Except your progeny require megadoses of humor. I used to think it was odd that the only women writing about homemaking and child raising were funny ladies: Jean Kerr and Erma Bombeck and Judith Viorst, all wonderful writers who let me know there was someone in the same boat even if it seemed to be sinking.

Eventually it dawned on me that it wasn't odd at all —it made perfect sense, because the only women who can take motherhood in their stride are those with a well-developed sense of humor. Which may explain another phenomenon, since I've never yet read or heard anything that would make me suspect that women's libbers have a funny bone. It's no wonder they had to get away from the house and kids. Without a strong inclination to laugh, especially at yourself, a full-time mother is more handicapped than a one-legged Tarzan.

Take, for instance, family squabbles. Dag Hammarskjöld would have become an iconoclast if he'd had to arbitrate the disputes a mother must settle. There are the garden-variety ones like who gets the wishbone or the car's window seat. But nothing is too insignificant for siblings to quarrel over. For years I spent part of each evening allocating the "hot end of the tub." To this day I know not which end was considered warmer, I just know it seemed awfully important at the time.

Grandpa O'Donohue had the perfect way to handle children's squabbles. He recited poetry. Now that may sound ineffectual, but hear me out. He recited the same poem each time:

> Whatever brawl disturbs the street
> There should be peace at home.
> Where sisters dwell and brothers meet
> Quarrels should never come.
> Birds in their little nests agree
> That it is a shameful sight,
> When children of one family
> Fall out, and chide, and fight.

Like Grandpa, I recite it slowly and always in its

entirety, and my children would rather surrender the window seat for a six-hour drive than have to listen to that poem one more time.

The biggest part of today's problems is that we know the problems. My grandmother wasn't told she might not be fulfilled and she could be oppressed. She thought she was liberated when Grandpa married her and took her out of that blouse factory. And if anyone had suggested that she had a stereotyped role, exploited by male chauvinism, she would have thought they were "not playing with a full deck."

She never worried about coping with sibling rivalry because she never heard of it. She never identified which was her middle child, so clearly she could not be expected to handle his problem. She had no experts to advise her about psychology so she was free to rely on her instincts, and they served her well. She never heard about "establishing interpersonal bonds" with her baby, but she did it. She breast-fed because it didn't make sense not to. It was cheap and convenient and gave her a chance to take a load off her feet. She also believed it might prevent conception, so she nursed each baby until the next was on its way. Being a good Catholic woman she accepted her pregnancies calmly, although she admitted that she wouldn't take a million dollars for the children she had and wouldn't give a nickel for another one.

After her seventh child, well into her forties, Grandma wasn't taking any chances. To the undying horror of her sister Molly, she nursed Eddie for so long that he took to fetching cookies before he jumped up on her lap.

CHAPTER

13

H AVE YOU NOTICED HOW MANY THINGS NO ONE EVER tells you? They exist, they're often universal truths, but for some unreasonable reason, in accordance with some unwritten law, you're obliged to discover them for yourself. Oh, they tell you everything else—usually quite more than you wanted to know—but they leave out some critical part of each experience and when you do finally learn it you're expected to keep it to yourself.

Not only has my recently acquired middle age failed to make me mellow, it's further diminished my chronically weak resolve to set a good example. I grow increasingly more like my friend Annie who always pleaded, "C'mon, tell me. You know I can keep a secret. It's just those loudmouths I tell it to who can't."

I'm turning into one of her loudmouths, no longer above spilling what no one ever told me. For instance, when you're expecting your first baby, you're advised about fetal development, the stages of labor, delivery procedures. Every mother you meet, however casually, details her gory experiences. But for some inexplicable reason, no one, no one (not even your own mother, which dramatizes the extent of the conspiracy) tells you that for a week after the baby is born your bottom is going to feel like you've just completed a nonstop trip across the Rockies on a bicycle with a loose seat.

Like most humans, I approached middle age tentatively. One might even say, reluctantly. But apprehensions were met with comforting and generally well-meaning advice. My doctor detailed female menopause, my aunts explained male menopause. My friends outlined the empty-nest syndrome and midlife crisis. If not forearmed, I was at least forewarned. Or thought I was. But then there were those things no one ever told me.

Look, I figured out that there were more years behind than in front of me, but I'd been assured that as a nonsmoking, nonalcoholic (for the minute) person, my body should last another quarter century. No one mentioned that after just forty short years the warranty on all my parts ran out. That pipes would begin to clog and I'd need all new washers. That eyes and ears become inept, gums less gummy and teeth wobbly. That as hair thinned and grayed, nature would attempt some perverse structural balance by doubling up on the chin. That a waist that heretofore had only stretched horizontally would suddenly begin inching up vertically (like a badly tuned TV picture), threatening a rather nasty collision with a simultaneously falling bust. And that knees would commence to malfunction, working well enough to lower me down but failing dismally to boost me back up again. I knew all these things happened eventually, but not so soon.

As if all of this wasn't disconcerting enough, something even more unforeseen began to happen. Downright spooky it was. I caught a glimpse of my face in the hall mirror and there on my forehead was my mother's frown. Not long after, I began to notice her hands sticking out of my sleeves.

Probably all this is because when I last saw Mama she was middle-aged and because we tend to imitate those we admire so I become more like her even as my eight-year-old mimics the Fonz. In any event, it was my menopausal *déjà vu* that triggered memories of the days when I was a small girl whose only exposure to being a woman was watching Mama and Grandma handle their lives. And I wonder why I still cling to their values when I am bombarded with so much exhortation to the contrary. And I compare my life with theirs and think how much better off I am and how much easier they had it. Like chocolate soufflés, women's lives today are richer but vastly more complicated than the pudding lives women had in simpler times.

It's been said that your first three to five years create the patterns within which you'll live your life, and I had blessed early years. The neighborhood in Brooklyn was hardly fashionable and our row house epitomized "unpretentious." But it was across the street from my grandparents' row house and therein lies the tale.

Mama was the oldest girl in her family of seven and was only nineteen when I was born, so her younger brothers and sisters weren't much older than I. Even when I was very small I could never get enough of being in Grandma's house, although each short trip meant standing on the curb shouting, "Cross me,

Grandma, cross me." Self-determination and budding independence came into my life the day I could navigate Foster Avenue unattended. And be with Grandpa and Grandma.

Grandpa was Mike O'Donohue, a fireman, chief of Ten Truck in lower Manhattan, and what the Irish called "a fine broth of a man." He was very old-fashioned and I never saw him in casual clothes even out of uniform. He wore a shirt and tie to mow his small lawn. And high black shoes whose shine never dimmed.

Grandpa never cussed. He didn't even say words like "virgin" or "pregnant," never mind the four-letter words thrown around today. But he had the Irishman's lively way with words which were vastly more expressive. My all-time favorite was his description of ugliness, which came in three stages. There was "homely as sin," "homely as mortal sin," and the ultimate, "homely as a bagful of assholes."

Grandpa was nothing if not frugal. He mended all the children's shoes, gave them haircuts and he saved everything. Each Christmas we all lined up around the dining room table and he handed out envelopes containing one or two dollars depending on your age. His son had once run a dance that must have been the biggest social flop in the history of Fordham University because hundreds of invitations were left over. Until he died in 1949, Grandpa's Christmas envelope contained an engraved card that read, "The Brooklyn Club of Fordham University invites you to its 1935 Spring Formal, etc., etc." Neatly printed (right under "Tickets $3 per couple") was, "And a Merry Christmas from Pop."

Grandma was Susie, Aunt Sue, Mrs. O'D. to the neighbors and the most loving and generous and funny woman I've ever known. Even her faults were appealing. She loved gossip and asked, like Mrs. Longworth, "If you have nothing good to say about anyone, come sit by me." In her last years, living in a small town with Mama, one of the things she missed most was the backyard gossip from the old neighborhood. But God was good and sent a couple into the house next door who livened things up. Their kitchen was only a few feet from Grandma's bedroom window and she got a new lease on life just listening to them fight. Her only complaint was that the husband was too soft-spoken, too hard to hear. One night when there was a particularly juicy battle going on, Grandma became so frustrated that she finally shouted out her window, "Speak up, Ernie. For God's sake, speak up." He did too. Why should she know only his wife's side?

Back in Brooklyn Grandma had been a very typical housewife, leading much the same life as her contemporaries. She brought up seven children and kept house. She cooked and cleaned and did the laundry once a week in a big tub with a wringer clamped to one end. And she harnessed solar energy to dry the clothes by pinning them on a line. She shopped every day at the corner grocery and the butcher's next door, and bought most of her fruits and vegetables from a peddler who came down the street twice a week. He was a dear little hunchbacked man she called Johnny Look-up and if he had another name we never knew it. And God help him if he ever sold Grandma a soft potato or a hard peach.

When the weather was bad the butcher and grocer would deliver your phoned-in order and the Dugan's man came by each morning with fresh bread and doughnuts. In later years Grandma went to the new supermarket but hated having to choose from all those confusing brands. She once asked a young clerk which was the best toilet paper and laughed out loud when he answered, "On the whole they're all about the same."

Back then, there were no frozen foods or instant potatoes, so the best part of each afternoon Grandma spent preparing dinner, and she was an inspired cook. She never possessed a cookbook or a recipe file. In fact she never used that word. Like Mrs. Bridges, she always said "ree-ceet," and did not own a calibrated cup or even a set of nesting spoons. She cooked from memory and instinct, measuring in handfuls and pinches, drops and smidgens.

Grandma cooked totally unencumbered by today's work-saving gadgets. She never had a coffee maker or a crepe maker or doughnut maker or toaster oven, or fearless fryer or crock pot. She had one appliance that did it all—a stove. A thing of beauty with long pale-green legs and a waist-high oven.

Grandma's one electric appliance was the refrigerator which replaced the old icebox right before I was born. It was sensibly placed not inside the hot kitchen but out in the pantry by the back door and had legs that kept it off the floor (and the drip pan) and a big, spiraling motor on top. And filled as it always was with the most marvelous treats, it was less an appliance than a life-support system. Grandma thoroughly enjoyed her "frig" after years of struggling with a messy icebox. As a bride in a five-story walkup, she'd watched the iceman stagger up one hot summer day with his heavy, dripping load only to have Grandpa shout, "Is that what you call a nickel piece of ice?"

When I think of Grandma's cooking the first thing that always hits me is what she didn't make. She did not make salads. Like most Irish, she was suspicious of uncooked vegetables and except for cucumbers in sour cream (and that's the whole recipe), salads were unknown. There was no French or Italian food and never a barbecue—a good thing because at family picnics Grandpa refused to man the grill, claiming he was trained to put fires out. And Grandma never made casseroles and did few sauces.

But she made breads and cakes, pies and puddings, and did wonderful things with the vegetables provided by Johnny Look-up. She did potato pancakes, mincing the potatoes on an old tin grater which claimed bits of her knuckles. And she made Welsh rarebits and pots of glorious soup from scraps and bones.

Dinner was eaten in the dining room and was usually a roast accompanied by two kinds of potatoes and several other vegetables. She spoiled her children shamelessly by never insisting they eat everything on their plates. Instead she used the most basic Irish trick: tell everyone what he wants to hear. She was so expert at this that even when her two older boys were in college she could get them both to eat the same meat by telling one it was ham and the other it was tongue. Dinner was a time everyone came together. Grandpa presided and said grace and when money was short

155

he admonished all present to "smell the meat and eat the bread."

Grandma's housework was fairly perfunctory and twice a year there was a complete spring or fall cleaning in which the entire family participated, with Grandpa in charge. Always the fire chief, he'd call out orders like, "All hands to the pump." And when the task was completed he signaled with, "Haul up the ladder, boys."

While everyone else carried out Grandpa's orders, Grandma was busy washing the lace curtains. Now she missed out on permanent press, but she had curtain stretchers, great contraptions left over from the Inquisition. They were huge frames edged with tiny spikes and guaranteed to dot your clean white curtains with your bright red blood.

Grandma worked hard, but in many ways today's housewives work harder. First, she had the security of knowing exactly what was expected of her while our duties are more complex. And she had much less frustration to handle because she was more in control of her life. She had no machines to deal with, *ergo* no repairmen, service contracts or time payments. All her appliances were hand-driven by her hand and the only dishwasher that occasionally acted up was Grandpa. She never wrestled with a vacuum—she had a carpet sweeper and a broom and a rug beater (Grandpa again).

I am not, believe me, trying to suggest that our grandmothers had easy lives. Just less complicated ones. The work housewives did years ago was backbreaking. In fact, all those hours on her feet gave

Grandma terrible varicose veins and eventually cost her one leg. In her seventies she got a wooden one and when asked which leg it was, she always told the truth —the good-looking one. Years after she died, her leg still stood in the corner of Mama's cellar, complete with stocking and shoe, giving quite a jolt to the meter reader and the plumber. I once asked my little nephew if he remembered Grandma O'Donohue and he said, sweetly, "No, but I knew her leg."

It was only right that Grandma lived with Mama until she died. No other arrangement was ever considered, for they came from a tradition of strong family ties and loyalties. Grandma never heard of the "extended family" or the "nuclear family." For most of her life she never lived farther than a trolley ride from her relatives. She belonged to a time when everyone took care of their own and in turn were cared for, when nursing homes were unheard of and the poorhouse was the last resort of the friendless.

Every time I hear about families who don't want anyone living with them because they'd miss their privacy, I think of Uncle Packy. Uncle Packy was Grandma's only brother and when he needed a place to live he came to her. She already had two or more children in every bed, so for three years Packy slept in the Morris chair in the front room. He tried to repay her kindness by giving a hand with repairs around the house and Grandma said he was a great help, but I rather doubt it. Certainly he meant well, but he died in 1939 and the kitchen chairs he varnished still haven't dried.

CHAPTER

I T SOMETIMES SEEMS THAT A PRIZE MUST HAVE BEEN offered to the American family who can most complicate their lives, and everyone is out to grab it. They start by taking a compass and figuring out on the map the farthest spot from the husband's place of work and then buying a home there. Extra points must be awarded for difficulty of commutation, with a ten-point bonus for those who use more than three modes of transportation in each direction: car, train, bus and subway are a winning combination.

In addition to buying a house as remote from the job as possible, they get more points in the Complicate-Your-Life sweepstakes if that house is also not within walking distance of any store, school or public transportation. There are points awarded for living in areas without sewers, sidewalks and drainage systems.

Once they are securely settled in such an area, the points for complicating begin to mount up in a dizzy-ing mathematical progression. Children are enrolled in dancing classes and Little League and midget football and Cub Scouts, and Mom gets to spend more time at the wheel than the average teamster. The town fathers decide that the area now needs sewers and sidewalks and drainage control and the taxes double. The financial strain becomes so great that the mother of the household must find a job and begin her own commute, plus coming home to chauffeur kids to doctors, dentists, school functions, lessons and all the other places they can't get to on their own.

Today's housewife has a fuller life than her grandmother did. On the average she is better educated, reads more and sees more of the world whether it be on television or from the window of the family camper. But her life is dramatically more complicated.

My grandmother never even owned a car, so there was never a question of holding up her end of a car pool or driving the children anywhere. Or driving herself anywhere. She didn't bowl, play tennis, golf or go to Weight Watchers. She didn't have a standing appointment at the hairdresser's, or, saints preserve us, the nail salon.

She never served on a committee or went to a meeting. She did not do volunteer work for any organization, but everyone on the block knew you could count on Mrs. O'D. She minded babies and listened to troubles and was a notoriously soft touch. When one neighborhood family was very down on its luck, Grandma cooked a big ham and asked Frankie to take it over to them. But first she sliced a few pieces off the end. "Tell them it was left over," she said, because she understood their pride as much as their hunger.

Without belonging to an organization or playing a sport, Grandma had no opportunity to compete with other women. In her day women got together to sew quilts or cook for the church supper. Now we are confronting each other, not only in the business world, but on the tennis courts and in bowling leagues. Grandma played cutthroat poker, but bridge was a social crux of many a pleasant afternoon where now it is played as duplicate in tournament halls.

It is a steady source of amazement to witness the importance some women put on competing today. Women with families, elderly parents, homes and often jobs, whose entire image of themselves seems to rest on their performance in bowling alleys or on the tennis courts. Women who would never push you in a crowded store would gleefully ram a tennis ball down your throat in the most insignificant local tournament. Women who would never take change for a ten when they'd paid with a five, will outright lie about a tennis ball's touchdown point. And if you could use a good laugh, close your eyes and try to imagine your grandparents or parents spending their vacation at a tennis camp.

If there was anything Grandma thought less of than competitions it was going to a doctor or dentist. I feel like I've spent half my adult life in doctors' waiting rooms, but in her day good dental care consisted of strong string and a solid doorknob. And doctors were an indulgence of the rich and generally regarded by her as unreliable quacks. Grandma's line was, "If you want a second opinion, I'll call a doctor." But she never did. She diagnosed your problem, prescribed treatment and administered same.

In truth, the Irish like most immigrants had small knowledge of medicine. Tetanus shots were undreamed of—they spit tobacco juice into open wounds. And nobody went for a physical examination unless it was required for a job. Uncle Marty drove a bus and the company demanded a yearly checkup. Once the doctor noted a problem and gave him suppositories to be used at bedtime. Months later Marty complained to Grandpa about the awful pills he'd been ordered to take. Said he, "Not only were they great huge things that I near choked trying to swallow, but for all the good they did I could have shoved them up my arse."

Grandma's medicines are easy to describe. Aspirin. That was it. Every ailment was cured with aspirin plus rest, God's good fresh air and food. For colds you were given a mixture of honey, lemon and Irish whiskey which didn't cure the cold but made you care dramatically less about having it. Almost any illness was met with beef tea, a strong broth make by boiling down large amounts of meat with a little water until you had a strong rich broth. At today's prices, liquid platinum would be more economical.

For congestion, or what Aunt Adelaide called "bronni-cal trouble," there was the mustard plaster. Grandma was the family authority here. She took a large piece of gauze and covered it with a thick spread of Colman's mustard (the powdered kind mixed with water to form a paste). It was then laid on your chest, gauze side down, and left there until it stopped burning or you vowed you'd recovered (which usually came first). One niece who called Grandma for instructions got it all straight except that she became confused about the last step and put the plaster, mustard side down, on her young husband's chest. For the rest of his life, he never had another cold or any hair on his chest either.

We have today hit the other extreme. No longer do the curative potions consist of food; food is now made from pharmaceuticals. I bought a tin of that European coffee mix guaranteed to impress your friends with the high level of your sophistication. The label listed eleven ingredients, each one of which sounded like something you'd scatter about to kill roaches. We now have nonfood foods made with artificial sugar, imitation colors, simulated milk and reprocessed flavors.

Years ago there was no such thing as health foods or natural foods. All food was good and the only problem was getting enough of it. No fretting about Red Dye Number Anything or polyunsaturated fats or cholesterol. When Grandma finally heard about cholesterol, she confused it with Musterole and never could figure why anyone would want to eat that stuff anyway.

There was no such thing as physical fitness. Anyone not crippled or deformed gratefully considered himself healthy. My grandparents never, never exercised: it didn't even occur to them. The only thing they knew about jogging was that it was good for the memory; if an adult ran it was in pursuit of a trolley or a purse snatcher. And only someone "gone mental" would sit on a bike and pedal away to nowhere. In her old age Grandma once stayed with a relative who, to her consternation, had not only a huge Exercycle but a sauna as well. And she'd invariably answer the phone, "Sonny can't speak to you right now. He's getting himself poached."

Grandma's recreation, sports, hobbies and outside interests can all be summed up in one word. Cards. She dealt like a riverboat gambler and played to win even with a four-year-old granddaughter being taught slapjack. Almost every night of her life, certainly after Sunday dinner, dishes were put away and the dining table cleared for cards.

Besides Grandpa, Grandma and Aunt Molly, there were always neighbors or friends dropping by for a game. There was one sweet old gentleman who came twice a month to be fleeced at pinochle. He was Molly's lifelong suitor, an accountant whose name I think was Alfred, but I never heard him called anything but "the old boob" (or to his face, "you old boob"). And it was a rare night when he left with more than the carfare home jingling in his pockets.

They played serious cards. Not much idle chatter. In fact the only sound you'd hear from the next room was the steady humming of Grandma and Aunt Molly. They sang bits of the few songs they knew—church hymns—interspersing them with brief comments on the trend of the game. So it was not unusual to hear a sweet old lady's voice quietly singing, "Holy God, we praise Thy name . . . damn . . . Lord of all . . . ante up . . . we bow before Thee . . . your deal."

In their eighties Grandma and Molly played endless canasta and every so often Molly would stop to recall some incident of their childhood which she was remembering with the clarity that often accompanies old age. Grandma, though, always cared more about the game and would finally squash Molly with, "If only you could remember who dealt last."

When Grandma was raising her children she never had much time even for the radio and I was full-grown before she got her first TV. It had a screen the size of *Reader's Digest* and a water-filled amplifier fit over it to enlarge the picture. Programs were all live then. Think of that. My children have spent half their lives being entertained by dead people. Between old movies and reruns and taping ahead, they have no conception of the usual order of aging. My daughter cried herself to sleep when she found out that the Shirley Temple she wanted for a best friend was forty-six years old.

The impact of television is one of the great changes in all our lives, but particularly so for housewives. A woman who stays at home most of the day can be just as well informed about world affairs as anyone in the business world. Often she is more knowledgeable. Yet TV falls short of being the housewife's best friend, because it is seldom geared to her needs.

To me, TV is wonderful and I have problems with people who call it the "boob tube" and tell you they never watch it because it's all trash. And then when you go to their homes there's a set in every room and you begin to wonder by what clairvoyant feat they know it's all trash if they never watch it. Truthfully, most of it is trash, but it can be awfully good.

If television often misses the boat, perhaps it is because network programmers don't give us what we want but what they think we want. We want to be entertained and they give us *Starsky and Hutch.* We want to be informed about the things that affect us and they give us the nightly news. The big problem with the news is that it's the same every night and the networks are wasting a lot of bucks by not running the news like they do the other shows—one-third of the year do original shows and then do two cycles of reruns. Who's to know? The network news always involves peace talks breaking down in the Middle East, inflation hitting an all-time high, renewed violence in Northern Ireland, New York City going bankrupt at midnight tonight, a tanker of Liberian registry going around spilling millions of gallons of oil into the sea.

Inserts could be implemented to update reports such as "The _____ Workers went on strike at midnight last night," this accompanied by stock footage of pickets carrying "Unfair" signs. I'd make book that if a network reran a six-month-old newscast and omitted the one-tenth of the program pertaining to blizzards or heat waves no one would be the wiser. And all those poor correspondents lunging around the world would get to spend some time at home with their families.

And then there's Saturday morning. The networks assume that only small children watch TV on Saturday mornings and so they fill the time with cartoons, thereby creating a self-fulfilling prophecy. Now, all week long men and women run off to work right in the middle of a *Today Show* interview or a *Good Morning America* report by Jack Anderson and dream of being able to see their favorite morning shows in their entirety. So why don't the networks rerun these programs in condensed form, leaving out the hard news, on Saturday mornings when an adult person with an I.Q. higher than fifty might be grateful to relax with his coffee and see what he missed.

There should be a law against the three national networks all showing the same thing, whether it's cartoons, a presidential news conference or a space shot. Prime times, whatever they are—Sunday night seems to be the primest—should be drawn for like the NFL draws for top college players. The networks would go around the table in an orderly manner, snagging the best spots—Thanksgiving night or whatever—for their station and other stations would have to stick to regular programming. Then, after a week of tripe, a family wouldn't have to decide between three good special programs all on at the same time.

And finally, obscenity is in the eye of the beholder, but I happen to find football games on Christmas Day immoral. If this nation is committed to the family, then the FCC should stop anything as destructive to family life as a televised football game on a national family holiday. Isn't it enough that many heads of households have had the bends every January 2 after too sudden withdrawal from A-to-Z bowl games?

There are endless Blue Ribbon panels discussing the violence on TV and its impact on our youth. But I have yet to view a series that could match the insensitivity of local news programs. It is my earnest prayer that the hotter spots in hell are reserved for television reporters who thrust microphones into the faces of the bereaved and ask questions like, "Are you going ahead with putting up your Christmas tree now that all your children just burned to death?"

There is so much we need to know about new laws affecting our lives, developments in health care and education, and television could be so good that it's a sin how much of it is bad. You hear it's destructive to family life because people forget how to talk to each other. Our experience has been quite the reverse. Maybe because nothing short of muzzles could keep us from talking. But some of our best family moments have been sitting around the TV watching the Olympics or the Kentucky Derby or the Watergate hearings or *The Odd Couple*.

Maybe it's because all of us sitting around watching

something together is just about our only stab at to-getherness. Of the many forces that can plague the American family, the most lethal is surely "together-ness"; everybody doing everything together and trying so hard to look happy about it. Pretending to enjoy the same things and wearing the forced expression Grandpa used to describe as "a smile like a wave in a slop bucket."

When Mama was first born her parents lived in a tenement on Bank Street in lower Manhattan. It was one room and had a small stove and icebox, and they shared toilet and bathing facilities with their neighbors and lived with the incredible noise and confusion that such closely packed humanity makes inevitable. People live that way today. They call it camping and do it for fun, to get away from their eight-room house on one acre with three bathrooms and an all-electric kitchen that Grandma would have thought was heaven.

Camping is the ultimate togetherness, but it is also my idea of the most foolproof way to break up a solid family. If the Waltons had taken up camping they'd be in Family Court. We've done it twice, in borrowed campers, but once was enough. Only someone with an advanced foot fetish could enjoy trying to sleep in a small space with six other people; every time you open your eyes, someone's toes are under your nose. Neither is it designed to strengthen marriage ties, because even in the best-designed campers, it becomes clear that the most fundamental sexual relations are remotely pos-sible only if you happen to have trained with The Fly-ing Tremendoes.

CHAPTER

15

I IS RUMORED THAT THE FAMILY IS NOT A VIABLE way of life in this modern world and that the Happy American Family was a myth anyway. The family may be changing, may be smaller and include more nonblood relatives, but it continues to function albeit often in disguise. The lure of communes and funky religions seems to be that they offer membership in a large supportive group, an alternative to the loneliness that is this generation's version of the Black Plague.

For we humans, like the elephant and the buffalo, are essentially herd creatures, functioning best in groups where we support, aggravate, encourage, embarrass and amuse each other. Nature saw to it that we cannot even tickle ourselves and many people can't laugh at themselves. The family fills basic human needs and despite prophets of gloom it appears to be surviving.

As for the myth of the Happy American Family, that depends on how you equate happiness. Grandma had no yardstick against which to judge her family's happiness quotient except what she saw around her. Next door was a lady married to a drunk and the neighbor on the other side had a sweet husband who couldn't hold a job. Grandma's relatives all had their share of problems and so, by comparison, her husband and children and their life together looked pretty good.

Today's families have more perfect models against which to measure their happiness. They are farther removed from neighbors and may live hundreds of miles from brothers and sisters, but they have those TV families serving as role models and all those commercials that portray them chuckling over hamburgers, crying for help and who took the dandruff shampoo. They have print ads of family gatherings, especially the Christmas ones, with parents, grandparents and spiffy children smiling at each other around the festive table.

And then they live the reality of their own Christmas dinner. Uncle George so plastered only the occasional rattle of his ice cubes suggests he's still alive. Aunt Lillian with circles of rouge, and lipstick touching her nostrils. Kids squalling, the man of the house hacking away at the overcooked turkey and Mom reflecting all the serenity of someone who has just fled a burning building.

Not one advertisement or feature layout ever seems to portray a realistic family gathering. Grandpa had cousins who resembled the cast of a Vincent Price movie. The wife looked like Bela Lugosi with a moustache and Mama's brother Frankie once gave the father of the group a big hug good-bye, explaining later that he was looking for bolts in his neck. It was that same Frankie, who years earlier as a very small boy, had greeted them at the door with, "My mother hoped you wouldn't come."

Every family, no matter the size, has at least one bore, one hypochondriac, one snoop, one critic and one poor (as in "Poor Herbie" or "Poor Alice"). We had several of each actually, plus a few who could chew your ear off. Uncle Willie who made pots of money never let us forget it. He flaunted his big car and at one family party when he offered to drive Grandma and Grandpa home, Grandpa said, "You already have."

In Mama's house there was always a profusion of priests. Dad's brother was, and is, a Jesuit missionary and there was an endless procession of men from his order dropping by with messages, requests and greetings. Someone once asked Dad if there was a term like rummy or wino for someone who only drank scotch, and Dad said, "Yes. A Jesuit."

In those days families always visited, usually unannounced, and in both Grandma's and Mama's homes company was the rule not the exception. And everyone brought something with him—liquor or beer, cake or pie. You would never go visiting empty-handed, "with one arm as long as the other."

There were an extraordinary number of get-togethers, particularly during the war when there were farewell and welcome-home parties always on the agenda. The menu was fairly predictable because each woman brought along her specialty, so you could count on Aunt Helen's potato salad, Agnes' soda bread, Aunt Mamie's pound cake, Lucille's meatballs, Aunt Molly's sardine spread and on it went.

The entertainment was also predictable since again everyone had a specialty. Mama sang about Molly Malone ("and cockles and mussels alive-alive-o"). Uncle Joe sang sad Irish songs about the "troubles" that made the old ladies cry and Uncle Frankie sang an Irish fighting song, the chorus of which went, "When resisting from the strife, best be a coward for five minutes than a dead man all your life."

Since most of the parties seemed to be at Grandma's house, there was always at least one round of "If You Knew Susie" and Uncle John did his imitation of James Cagney's imitation of George M. Cohan. At one party things got so out of hand that Dad finally said, "Anyone who wants to hear John do another chorus of 'Yankee Doodle Dandy' can signify by going home." Uncle John is sixty now and still brings down the house with "You're a Grand Old Flag," and Uncle Joe is almost seventy and there's not a dry eye in the place after his rendition of "I'll Take You Home Again Kathleen."

Like every family, ours always had its rituals and traditions and every holiday was thoroughly celebrated, but no excuse was too small for a get-together. Your family rejoiced with you at christenings and grieved with you at wakes. A funeral in the family often brought out people you thought were already dead. We had some relatives I wouldn't recognize unless they were decked out in black, perched on folding chairs.

Wakes were held at home and good people brought food and whiskey and everyone reminisced and cried and laughed. The one thing rarely spoken about at wakes was the cause of death. The Irish believed in ghosts, leprechauns and the power of prayer; they did not believe in illness. I recall hearing that Uncle Dinny met his maker on account of "shortness of breath" and when someone asked what Uncle Packy died of the answer was, "Nothing serious." A friend told me that when she asked what her Irish grandfather died of the reply was, "He died of a Tuesday."

When I was a little girl not only were wakes held at home, but everything was done at home—weddings, parties, entertaining, caring for the sick and the old. It always seemed odd that families started doing fewer things at home after they began building houses with family rooms. And it is astounding how much effort and money some people put into decorating their living room so that guests can get a glimpse of it on their way downstairs to the finished basement. What they end up with are nonliving rooms adjacent to nondining rooms and all too often a big expensive house never really becomes a home.

Grandma's house was small and had one bathroom for nine people and no one had his own room or even his own bed. There was no powder room, wet bar, patio or deck. There was a small backyard and a stoop. How we loved the stoop; you could sit all day watching your world go by.

But that small cramped house was a beautiful home because there was a housewife who made it so, and while any number of people can form a household, only one special person can create a home. In those days, too, a home was more of a necessity. For one thing, home used to be the only place you could get comfortable. Men rushed there to pull off heavy shoes and tight collars; children to strip off the school clothes in which they were forbidden to play or eat ice cream. And no matter how delightful the outing, every woman looked forward to getting home to take off her girdle.

I came of age in the era of the rubber girdle. Some profoundly disturbed woman hater perfected them. Although at the time they served a unique need because the only great sensual pleasure allowed to me as an unmarried Catholic girl was peeling off that rubber girdle. And can we ever forget when my mother-in-law's rubber girdle split and she made her husband take it to the gas station to be vulcanized? We laughed, but with that big red patch it tortured for another two years.

Home was also the only place you ate. We even came home from school for lunch. Fast-food chains were unheard of and eating out was just not done in our social circle. Once a year Aunt Molly treated the family to dinner in a restaurant. Actually it was the back room of the neighborhood tavern, and we all trooped through the ladies' entrance and were forbidden to peek into the bar. And Mrs. Shanley served corned beef while Mr. Shanley ("Himself," she called him) brought pitchers of beer for the adults and "pale dry" for the kiddos. And that was the closest we came to *haute cuisine*. And I never enjoyed a restaurant more.

Except for that yearly excursion to Shanley's, the social event of the week was Sunday dinner at Grandma's. She prepared a feast even though often that meant "chicken on Sunday and feathers all week." Aunt Molly arrived about three in the afternoon with a shopping bag containing several liquor bottles and a cocktail shaker (and a determination to ruin dinner, according to Grandpa).

There was always company. Anyone in the family could and did invite friends, and Grandma took it in stride. When I give dinner parties and work for days preparing fancy hors d'oeuvres and a gourmet meal, I envy Grandma who readied for guests by putting extra potatoes in the oven. When I find myself pondering the correct wine to serve, I'm jealous of Grandma who gussied up for company by putting ice in the water glasses. And when I sit at fancy dinner parties where the host is restless and ill at ease, I remember Grandpa and how contented he was as he looked around his crowded table and loudly announced, "Oh, if these good times would only last."

Our mobile society and shifting values have made those big Sunday family dinners a thing of the past. In fact, big families appear to be a thing of the past, and what a pity, for no situation is more conducive to teaching a child how to get along in life than being brought up in a large family.

The rewards are many and varied and there are mixed blessings—heavy on the mixed blessings. There are little things like never sitting on a cold toilet seat and big things like always having someone to talk to and borrow from and blame. Now someone to blame is no small thing and fills a profound human need. One of life's great lessons taught in family situations is that the one who can smile when things go wrong is the one who has thought of someone he can blame.

So when things went badly you could always decide

it was because your brother kept you awake the night before or your sister ruined the good dress that would have made a better impression. How much simpler life was when your every setback or failure could be laid at someone else's feet.

Today, robbed of this coterie of live-in scapegoats, we are forced to place our blame elsewhere. This need has given rise to a whole new category of books that show you how your troubles are still not your fault. They are along the lines of "Our Mothers, Our Enemies," "Your Children Stunt Your Growth," "The Role of Marriage in Hypertension" and "Fluoridated Water— The Key to Hostility."

If you get caught in a scandal or a crime, you can write a book telling how it really wasn't your fault. The only catch being that if the scandal is big enough everyone involved writes a book putting himself in the best light, and the various versions acquire a Rashomon-like quality that can make you look foolish and/or slap you in the slammer.

So we've compensated for someone to blame, and as for the someone to talk to, that's been taken care of too. To fill the void of not living among a big family we have contrived encounter groups and group therapy. Hundreds of generations of families provided group therapy of the best kind, where no one had to be paid to listen. The therapy was uncomplicated since neurosis had not yet been perfected so you couldn't get one. Also there wasn't time to dwell on small problems or imagined slights; you were too busy with big problems and real slights.

Large families automatically provided perpetual encounter. They saw to it that the things you learned most about were your own shortcomings. You confronted them regularly because they were what identified you. If you had an overbite you were "Bucky" or "Beaver." Unusual heights required "Gawk" or "Peanuts," and there was "Skinny," "Bones," "Fatso" and "El Flabbo." At a recent family reunion a fine-looking man came over and said, "Don't you recognize me? Applehead Feeney?"

Those were the days of "Blondie" and "Blackie" and "Red." But mostly, throughout the family, your imperfections were your claim to fame. A perfectly nice young man, an A student and varsity track star, was "Aunt Ella's boy with the ears like a loving cup." And the question was often asked, "Which would you rather have, a hundred dollars or Freddie's nose full of nickels?" There was Aunt Fanny whose eyes gazed at each other with undisguised puzzlement and of whom it **was** often said, "But she didn't ask me. She asked you." Uncle Charlie, periodically institutionalized for megalomania (he was your classic Caesar, Napoleon, FDR), was known as "Crackers."

As kids, on long car rides we used to play Who Am I? and the questions were substantially more revealing than the answers. Are you older than Grandpa? Fatter than Aunt Essie? Shorter than Cousin Henry (about whom Frankie had once asked, "Is he a man or a boy?")? Are you someone we know? Are you famous? Are you anyone Uncle Charlie thought he was?

I didn't know much about other families, but ours always seemed special. Perhaps because as Macaulay said, "The Irish are distinguished by qualities which tend to make men interesting rather than prosperous." Also, our clan was made up of very kind people who cared about each other and offered a security to the children that no amount of money could have bought. Not everyone is as lucky, although families generally are a microcosm of the world. There are members who pick you up and some who put you down. There is envy and love, caring and greed.

In my family the greed revolved mostly around food, and many a fight erupted over attempts to tuck away some treasured goody. It's a fact of life that children who don't notice three 20-gallon garbage cans needing to be carried to the curb can find a Milky Way wrapped in old foil at the bottom of the freezer chest. Uncle Frankie, who was a bit of an innovator, got good results from putting notes on top of his snacks saying, "Don't touch. I spit on this." Until the day he found a strange scrawl at the bottom of his note saying, "So did I."

A particularly revealing episode happened one Sunday when twelve of us sat around the table and Mama brought out a dozen eclairs she'd bought as a special treat. When we heard a car door slam, my kid brother ran to the window and yelled, "It's Father Quinn. Quick, everybody, take a bite out of your eclair."

The family saw to it that before you were four feet tall you had mastered the finer points of survival. With food and with almost everything else. You learned that every group is ruled by its worst-tempered member; that the family clown gets away with murder; that there's always one pet and everyone knows it but him; that no good deed goes unpunished.

The family also taught the intricacies of "enlight-ened self-interest" at an early age, because hand-me-downs gave you a vested interest in your older brother's vested suit. You rooted for him not to trip and fall (and tear) and not to spill tea in his lap, and you were more disappointed than he when he failed to grow taller one year.

Grandma didn't face the frustration of going into a department store in June to buy a bathing suit and finding only fall clothes. She rarely shopped for clothes at all since she sewed the children's things herself and never threw anything out. Instead of the hassle of shopping, Grandma and Mama had one day each fall and spring when they cleaned closets and redistributed clothing, and everything they tried on you was de-scribed as "very nearly new." It got to be a standing joke—"Mama's nearly new."

In addition to your older siblings' duds, there were bonuses. Dapper Cousin Henry died leaving a closet full of good tweeds and flannels which were a veritable bonanza, and when I asked one of my brothers if that swell jacket came from "Mama's nearly new," he said, "Nope. Henry's hardly dead." We all prayed that wherever Henry was he was having half as good a time as his clothes.

The unfair part of hand-me-downs was that the youngest child was a virtual ragamuffin. Unless he was sneaky. Grandma's Eddie "borrowed" his older brother's new clothes and wore them to high school, and he might have gotten away with it if his graduat-ing class hadn't voted him Best Dressed.

There were no garage sales back then because nothing of possible value got thrown out. There was always a taker for a warm coat or shoes with some wear left in them. Often Grandma was given things by more affluent neighbors to send to "the poor Irish." Grandpa tried them on his children first, claiming, "There are few poorer Irish than ourselves." But at one point, in the early part of World War II, Grandpa set about collecting clothing for Greek relief on behalf of a dear man who ran the restaurant next to his firehouse. He called each relative, carefully explaining the situation in Greece, then asking, "And do you have any old tuxedos? You know they're all waiters."

Mama was a saver, too, coming by the trait honestly. As they used to say, "She didn't lick it off the stones." She kept her huge cedar closet filled with castoffs. When her priest cousin, Father Jim, was going on his first trip to Ireland, he had no decent civilian clothes (in those days priests in mufti tended to dress like racetrack touts). But he had some decent slacks, so Mama took him up to the closet and outfitted him with several tweed jackets, remnants of those heavy tweed suits Dad used to wear before the lighter blends proved more comfortable. Father Jim went off to Ireland armed with the addresses of all the relatives Mama had been corresponding with and sending packages to for years, and he visited every one. He said later those visits were the best part of his trip. He felt so at home because in every house he entered there was some fellow wearing trousers that matched his jacket.

CHAPTER

16

PLAIN TALK SEEMS TO HAVE DISAPPEARED WITH Harry Truman (or Harry Tru-person if that's your thing). This is the age of the euphemism. The poor are "culturally disadvantaged," the old are "senior citizens" who go to "health-related facilities" instead of nursing homes. Chicken wire is advertised as "poultry netting" and death is a word to avoid at all costs. So many people told me they were sorry I lost my mother, I suspected they thought we'd misplaced her. And then there were the ones who said, "And when did your mother expire?" (like some old credit card). Or, "So Mother is no longer with you" (she wasn't against us either).

Hand in hand with euphemisms are the words designated to indicate a concept but which are so undescriptive as to be ludicrous. For instance the word "gay" used to describe people whose life-style leaves them open to ridicule and cruel jokes. "Layette" seems a particularly unfortunate term for the necessities of a woman expecting a baby. A young man entering the army and embarking on barracks life is the last person on earth who deserves to be called "private." And couldn't they be "anti-moth balls," if only to dispel uncomfortable images of neutered insects?

"Housewife" is another such word, denoting a woman wed to a house. Terms like "domestic engineer" and "home manager" seem contrived and the eighteenth-century "goodwife" is not likely to catch on again. I rather like "homemaker" because that is what such women are all about—making beds, making meals, making love, making do. They are making a home for the most important family that ever was.

The American housewife is the most ingenious of women. She keeps appliances running long past their time with a combination of wire, tape and sheer will-power. She can repair, refinish or refinance almost anything. With less time and more distractions than her mother had, she is probably a better cook and house-keeper. She can work like a galley slave all day and go out that night looking like a duchess. Never has more been expected of her and never has the house-wife/homemaker been more undervalued.

Call it homemaking or housewifery but call it un-popular. It involves making other people's welfare your life's work and coolies were better paid; and those who would engage in it are not only marching to a different drummer, but one hopelessly out of tune with the beat of the times.

Dr. Schweitzer got in just under the wire, for clearly today self-sacrifice is out and self-absorption is in. People everywhere are asking themselves, "Am I ful-filled?" "Am I happy?" "Am I relating?" They are spending their lives trying to figure out where it hurts. We are, according to sociologists, in the "Me decade," with narcissism running amuck. Where once it was honorable to give your life to the care of others, it is now considered plain stupid. Even the most dedicated and effective volunteers find themselves viewed with skepticism and pressured to demand pay.

The final nail in the housewife's coffin was probably driven in by the admonition from Houston that she is only a husband away from welfare. That was a jolt. But then I figured, who isn't in that unfortunate position? Every worker is just a pink slip away from the unemployment line. Most small (and some big) businessmen are often perilously close to bankruptcy. The only exception that comes quickly to mind are schoolteachers with their treasured tenure, but even they are starting to worry.

Now I don't have tenure, but I do have one edge that has historically been a weighty advantage (forgive me Gloria Steinem); I sleep with the boss. I also know the date of his mother's birthday and the name of the only starch that doesn't give him hives. And how much Tabasco goes into his bloody marys. And I love his children as much as he does. It's not tenure, but it gives me clout.

Housewives are often as scorned as lepers because they would raise children instead of their consciousness; because they are more concerned with the development of their families than their potential. Our local newspaper printed a survey of the fifty most-admired occupations and at the bottom of the list were TV repairmen. But housewives weren't even on the list, which speaks volumes for the status of the world's second-oldest profession.

What always comes to mind when I try to explain how I feel about being a housewife is the time President Kennedy was shot. It was a tragic thing for his family and had great historic implications, but he had the most important job in the world and within hours another President had been sworn in and the government still functioned.

Not long afterward, my mother died in an accident. She was an average housewife with four children still living at home and no amount of help ever replaced her. Dad got a housekeeper but she didn't prepare meals, so I went across the street each night to fix dinner. One of my aunts took charge of the mending and ironing and my brothers did chores like defrosting the freezer and taking the dog for shots. At one point I realized that it took six of us to do what Mama had done with one hand (she usually had the phone in the other hand).

My mother and grandmother never thought of themselves as "role models," but they were to me and because of them I never considered homemaking as insignificant. How could I when these housewives were the most important members of our world? And many women who wrote to me said they felt the same way; that as homemakers they were central to their family's happiness and well-being and were doing the only job on earth they could do better than anyone else.

One of the most popular arguments used to convince women to work outside the home is that otherwise they are wasting their education. Yet no one tells a male college graduate he shouldn't take over his father's hardware business because he's wasting his education. Is education held in such low regard that it is desirable only for its value in the marketplace? I once read a line about when you educate a man, you educate a man, but when you educate a woman, you educate a family. And Phyllis McGinley agreed that housewives more than any other group deserve well-furnished minds—they have to live in them such a lot of the time.

I received hundreds of letters from well-educated and resourceful women who find their roles as home-makers very satisfying. Many plan to resume careers when their children are older, but many are content to center their lives on home, family and community. Their wishes, their life-styles, are just as valid as those of their sisters who choose to go off to a job. They are not staying home because of lack of confidence or initiative but out of free choice, having considered the possibilities and the advantages.

Perhaps the biggest thing a full-time homemaker has going for her is time. She is not tyrannized by the clock and is often able to arrange a few hours for herself or extra minutes with her husband and children. And in the long run, isn't time the one thing no one ever gets enough of?

Nothing is much fun when you're pressed for time. But when you can do things leisurely, and on your own schedule, simple chores can feed the soul. People will say, "I'd be bored stiff working around the house—fixing meals, mending, taking care of the yard." And then they tell you about the hobbies they wish they had more time for like cooking, needlework and gardening.

I've never found homemaking boring. Exhausting

and frustrating, but never boring. To keep a house running smoothly, clean clothes at the ready, food in the frig, surroundings comfortable, is the most challenging job imaginable. And the opportunities for creativity are endless. The satisfaction of refinishing a table or upholstering a chair or making an attractive arrangement out of a bunch of dried weeds is doubled because you have created something you will enjoy for years, while professional craftsmen are forced to sell their creations. It's the same with preparing meals. Chefs find satisfaction in cooking and they don't even have the pleasure of watching customers enjoy the food.

I've never been one who saw much merit in making cute things out of old hangers and empty toilet-paper rolls, but it's fun to frame a pleasing picture or make a lampshade out of cardboard, glue and some old lace. And it's a bigger thrill than yelling "Bingo" when you find a wicker chair or an old Victorian table in your neighbor's garbage.

Just about the only person I know who gets to do her own thing today is the housewife. I get to work at my own speed, in an environment of my own creation, among people of my own creation. I get to squeeze in a nap when I'm weary, take a walk on a spring day, have lunch with a friend and occasionally work out a free afternoon for a museum trip or lecture. Since everyone knows about women's work, I can afford to leave undone as much or little as I choose.

I also have time for my friends and for some entertaining. So many housewives who wrote said that once their friends went to work, they rarely saw them again.

One New Jersey housewife said, "Oh, to be invited to a dinner party again." For it seems that whatever the circumstances, when a housewife's going out to work, the one thing she usually won't find enough time for is her friends. Now that is a great loss.

Liberated ladies talk a lot about being "sisters" and that always does me in because where I came from "sisters" wore black habits and frowns and were only slightly less frightening than the Wicked Witch of the North. But if you want to talk about sisterhood, nothing can compare with what Mama used to call "the wives' union." As a mother and housewife I have never found other housewives anything but supportive and kind. They'll swap recipes and favors, take over when the flu knocks you cold and bring casseroles when you have a death in the family. They'll lend you plates and pots and a hand when you're having a party, even if they're not invited. They'll keep an eye on your children and fetch you when your car is disabled in the supermarket parking lot. And won't ever tell a soul that you were the one who backed into the Salvation Army bin.

Like many of my "sisters," I suppose I was as made for housework as Kareem Abdul-Jabbar was made for basketball. The few really rotten aspects of housekeeping have disappeared and if I had a vote, I'd nominate for the Nobel prize whoever invented the self-cleaning oven. First runner-up would be the discoverer of frost-free refrigerators. Mama's first freezer was so bad we used to have to chisel things out, and every time she sent one of the kids down to fetch something from it he'd bring back "greetings from Nanook."

Technology has made the housewife's lot a happier one in terms of eliminating the grueling chores. Parts are still dreary, but even they have compensations. Rote jobs like dusting and bedmaking and folding laundry give you time to think, quiet time. Hardly a small treasure in this frantic world, especially for a wife and mother who is by definition fragmented by the variety of her obligations. When her days were most hectic, Mama would go to mass every morning, partly to pray for strength, I suppose, but often just to be quiet and alone.

It seemed like the older Mama got, the less solitude she had. I was out of her house only three years when I returned with a husband and two and a half children, and Grandma had come to live with her about the same time, so the total count was thirteen and a half and peaked at fifteen. We Hekkers didn't live in Mama's house, but had asked to use the rooms over her garage for a year while Jack got his law practice started. Six years later we were still there. Next time you're in a garage look around and try to imagine what it would be like living there with five other people—welfare wouldn't allow their most destitute client to have such cramped housing.

Finally Dad, who was one to call a spade a spade (or more likely "a goddamn shovel"), came up, looked around at our four children sleeping toe to toe, two in a bed, and said to my husband, "Hekker, you're screwing yourself right out of this place."

With that indelicate truth ringing in our ears, we hocked everything and bought a house. Somewhat lacking in the pioneer spirit, we purchased the house right across the street. Our new home was about one hundred years old and had been on the market for two years, advertised as a "handyman's special." Even the most optimistic realtors admitted it needed work. Jack's parents gave their verdict. "How could you pay thirty thousand dollars for a dump like that?" Mama, an eternal optimist, pronounced it "interesting" and my father said, "You're out of your friggin' minds." Our friends assured us the place had all the innate charm of an unsuccessful nursing home. The mortgage officer at the bank said, "If you want to get a V.A. loan, you'd better take another picture of the house and this time try to get more trees in the way." The exterior was bad, but inside was a disaster. The last renovation had been done in the mid-thirties in a style most kindly described as "late Carole Lombard."

But we would not be discouraged. Like most optimism, ours was founded on a solid base of stupidity. Just as with our marriage and the children, we didn't have the foggiest notion of what we were letting ourselves in for. We had given little thought to the fact that when you move from a three-room apartment to a fourteen-room house you are left eleven rooms short of furniture.

Those were the days before secondhand furniture was called "antiques," so we raced ahead of garbage trucks on pickup days and hounded junkyards. Ours was the only house in the neighborhood where the junkman delivered. Actually we were ahead of our time because we were recycling before the word was invented. We taught ourselves to re-upholster; I held while he tacked and I had two black thumbs for a year. Drapes were made out of bed sheets and old tablecloths and the final result was "homey."

Actually it all worked out well enough that our house has been used in over fifty television commercials. Not the fancy-shmancy kind where they serve Harvey's Bristol Cream, but the down-home kind where the husband says, "You know we can't afford expensive desserts," and the wife tells him it cost just nine cents a serving so he kisses her. In our kitchen a boy was saved from communicable disease by using a paper cup and a woman used her new electric oven to cook a magnificent turkey (stuffed with cotton and glazed with liquid Joy—that's show biz!). In the parlor an elderly couple smooched away secure in the knowledge that their dentures were held in place by the proper adhesive and Mark Twain regretted that he was born too late to use a certain loose-leaf folder.

In the den a young mother admonished her son to "Look it up in your own Funk and Wagnalls" (a line which by the twentieth take was absolutely obscene). In the bathroom a man in a striped robe felt his mouth come alive after using the best red mouthwash, so he began to dance. And a guy shaving wheeled toward the john and said, "I heard a plop" (it was his morning tomato juice).

Last summer children grouped around a piano on our porch and sang about the "best darn burger in the whole wide world" and in the fall an entire family celebrated Thanksgiving in our dining room while ignoring a pitiful waif who stood in the background representing world hunger.

The most memorable commercial happened years

ago. It was for an insurance company and involved a birthday party for a little black boy named Wendall. Our Tommy was going to be three that same week and when he came downstairs one morning to find prop men blowing up balloons and wrapping packages, nothing could convince him it wasn't for his birthday. Then the children arrived and he was shocked because they weren't his friends. And when they assembled around the festive table, there wasn't even a place for him. The crew felt so bad that they saved candy and favors for use at his party the next day. They even saw to it that the "prop" cake (real but not as large as the one actually used) was not touched so that he could have that too. Thank heaven only three-year-olds came to the party. It never dawned on them that Tommy's cake said, "Happy Birthday, Wendall."

CHAPTER

THERE ARE CERTAIN LIES WE'RE ALL TOLD AS CHILdren. Then we grow up and discover they're deceptions, but for some inexplicable reason we repeat them as facts to our children. There are the common ones like, "Good things come in small packages" (small things come in small packages). "It hurts me more than it hurts you" (no way!). There's "Tell the truth and shame the devil" (and get a slap in the face). "A friend in need is a friend indeed" (a friend in need is a pain in the ass).

The Irish had some doozies. There was, "Talk back to your mother and your hand will stick up in the grave." And a real winner, "Sew on Sunday and before you can go to heaven you'll have to pull the stitches out with your nose."

The afterlife notwithstanding, few subjects were more lied about than money. "Money is the root of all evil." "Money is dirty." "Money can't buy happiness." The truth is money is unimportant only to those who have never been without it, because happiness is just about the only thing it can't buy.

The best things in life (like health and fresh air)

are free, but the tragic things (like sickness and death) cost a bundle. There is no calamity that strikes where money can't cushion the blow. Illness, handicapped children, however heavy the cross is to bear, the lack of money adds to the burden. And having money lightens any load.

Money takes care of medical bills, undertakers, therapists and pharmacists. It buys higher education for your children, music lessons and straight teeth. Money has even been known to buy respect, friends and an occasional spouse.

In the British Museum there is a wing devoted to letters from great men—Michelangelo, George Washington, the Duke of Wellington (almost everyone Uncle Charlie thought he was). And the letters for the most part are not about philosophy, art or politics. They are along the lines of those we get from our children away at college: Send money. Michelangelo complained to the pope that the Carrara marble works refused to give him any more credit; George Washington was facing mutinous troops because the Continental Congress was slow with a buck, and Wellington had to plead with George III to pick up his tab at the Waterloo Inn.

Not long before she died, Grandma Moses was interviewed on TV by Ed Murrow and told about how many months it took to do one painting and how she used familiar scenes and the people close to her as models. Murrow suggested that she probably hated to part with a finished painting, and Grandma Moses smiled sweetly and said, "I'd rather have the money."

No one with any claim to maturity could honestly dispute the value of money. The trick is using it well and not paying too high a price for anything. Is the small inheritance you'll get from Uncle Walter worth letting the old poop ruin your holidays? Is the promotion worth uprooting your family? Is a fancy house worth both of you working night and day to pay for it? Is a job taken to make money for extras worth leaving your infant in the care of strangers?

There are countless young mothers who must work to support their children and themselves. There are women abandoned by their husbands, divorced and widowed, who have total responsibility for their children, and they are entitled to every break, every advantage our society can offer.

But many young mothers are working to provide their children with things they don't need. No baby is happier or healthier because he travels about in a fancy carriage or has his own yard. A baby is content anywhere he is loved and cared for and can be just as comfy in a blanket-lined laundry basket by an open window.

The most expensive toys sit on shelves as little ones play endlessly with measuring cups, egg poachers, wooden spoons and empty boxes. And they are singularly unimpressed with high-rent districts and expensive houses. Our first four babies were raised in tiny apartments, but Tommy came right from the hospital to a big house and yard. Recently, when I pointed out how lucky he was, he told me he'd really always wanted to live over one of the stores downtown where he could lean out the window and wave to his friends.

Children don't understand money. It's a relative thing to them. A rich person is one with more than they have and a poor person is one with less, and in the long run children need their parents' attention more than they need a ten-speed bike or their own TV.

For parents who really want to give their children "everything," may I recommend the ultimate gift. Grandparents. They offer more affection than a pony or a puppy and more security than five trust accounts. No one will ever love them more or be as devoted or understanding. It has been noted that the great bond between grandparents and grandchildren is that they share a common enemy. And it's true that some adults want to get away from parents who treat them like children (perhaps with good cause). But they care. And grandparents can give a child a sense of assurance and continuity that will enrich his whole life and his children's lives.

What picture is more touching than that of an old man baiting a hook for his small grandson or an old woman reading to her little granddaughter? Who but a grandparent will tell the world that your chubby little girl with braces is the most beautiful child alive and that your klutzy son playing third string for the Little League is such a pitcher the Yankees are after him already? And the beauty part is that they not only say it, they believe it.

On a more practical level, for a working mother, nearby grandparents can be lifesavers by mitigating the guilt she feels at leaving a sick child or not being able to clap for his performance as Mr. Tooth Decay in the school play. And dealing with guilt has always been a problem for working mothers, coming often from society but usually from within themselves. The guilt thing is not yet as dead as it deserves to be. Children never feel guilty about the demands they make of parents, so why should any parent feel guilty about doing what he or she must do to support a family. Yet our children always knew that a garage sale at a house with a working mother would be a bonanza of unused toys and unopened games.

Most working mothers have nothing to feel guilty about, whatever the reasons for going out to work, and in almost every case their children are the main beneficiaries. They are better housed and fed and have greater educational opportunities because their mother is breaking her neck to help provide for them. It is a rare household today that can get by on only one income. Most families eventually need two incomes to cover the necessities and almost all need two incomes if there are to be any extras. Because the truth is that no one in our economy is more financially overburdened than the middle-class family.

Lip service is given to the family as the strength of this nation, but the tax breaks go to the oil companies. We hear that the family is being weakened by materialism, women's liberation and divorce, but the truth is that all of them combined are not as threatening as our national policy and tax structure.

Living together has a tax advantage over marriage. Older couples must avoid legal marriage lest they have to forfeit some precious Social Security monies. We have the obscenity of a man divorcing his wife so that she is eligible for needed medical care and men forced to abandon their families to enable them to receive welfare benefits.

The welfare system is blatantly anti-family. If my

husband abandoned me today (and since I've been working on this book the possibility has grown less remote) welfare would pay me X dollars to care for my children. If I am not able to do it—and several trained nutritionists found it impossible to adequately feed individuals on welfare allotments—my children can go to a foster home where the government will pay 2X per child to a foster mother. If she can't handle it, they can go to an institution where the government will pay 3X per child. But they won't give me that much to care for my own child, no matter how much better off he is in the care of his own mother.

The tax deductions per child are a joke and the most routine dental and medical care presents an enormous burden to average parents. The single-family house, traditionally the specific dwelling of the family with children, is the most overtaxed item in this country. To strengthen the economy, farmers are paid subsidies and big corporations are bailed out of bankruptcy, but there are no subsidies to those who raise children—no one interested in bailing out financially pressed families.

There are many mothers who go out to work because they thoroughly enjoy it and find fulfillment there. There are many who are so enormously talented that it would be almost sinful for them not to pursue careers. Any woman, though, however large or small her gifts, is entitled to have any job she can qualify for and to make any arrangements necessary for the care of her family. This is her right.

Many mothers who go out to work do so because there is no way they can get by on just the husband's income. They may not be ready to get a job, they may not want to go out to work, to be away from their children, but they are forced into the job market by the outrageous cost of supporting their children. And whereas the government has begun to take steps to aid the mother who wants to work with tax deductions for baby-sitters and subsidized day care, no allowances are given to a mother who feels she wants to stay home with her young children. Which is just as much her right.

In Scotland years ago, an attempt was made to do all the weaving of fine woolens in factories with large machines, but it was soon learned the product was often inferior to the cloth woven by the hands of individual craftsmen. So the Scots wisely set up a system wherein weavers could work in their own homes, at their own looms, and still be part of a large organization that would market their goods and cover their medical and pension requirements. They called it "cottage industry" and it's been functioning successfully for decades.

Perhaps our government might be persuaded to dub child raising a "cottage industry" and give the mother who thinks she can do a better job of it raising her children in her home some of the benefits it accords those mothers who go out to work.

The same theory might be used to subsidize home care of the aged and handicapped. Parents of handicapped children who want to keep them at home, although they require expensive medication and therapy, get almost no allotments from the government. But when they are forced to institutionalize their child, the state pays anywhere from ten to thirty thousand dol-

lars a year for his care. The same rule applies to care
of the elderly, forcing families to institutionalize members they can't afford to keep at home.

This policy has made the American system of care
for the aged a national disgrace. In Australia they have
something called "Granny flats." When your older relative is no longer able to live independently, the government will put up a small prefab bungalow in your
backyard for them. It has a sitting room, bedroom,
kitchen and bath, all geared to people no longer agile,
and comes with almost all the things an elderly person might require. When we spoke about this idea
one night at the dinner table, Tommy said, "It would
be really nice if it came with a cat." Cat or not, it is
more humane and sensible than most nursing-home
care.

It is probably asking too much for our government
to make sense in this most insane of worlds. Nothing
makes sense when every day we hear about the situation in Northern Ireland where Irishmen kill each
other in the name of the Prince of Peace; in a world
where Jews and Arabs must war over possession of
holy lands; where public utilities are rewarded for
gross inefficiency by being granted higher rates to
cover their costs; where the richer a man is the less
likely he is to pay taxes; where the official government
comment is "Oops" when an eighty-million-dollar
satellite drops to the bottom of the Indian Ocean
while my neighbors go door to door trying to raise
money for cancer research; where our children are
graduating from high school lacking the most basic
skills while we are paying the highest school taxes in
the history of the world.

Women were not immune from all this, although perhaps it's only temporary insanity for them—a kind of amnesia from which they'll recover and then remember the place they've really earned in this world. Historically men may have been the great explorers, but women brought civilization. Women contributed order and beauty, morality and stability. Men may have found this country, but it was settled by women, because traditionally women had their priorities in good order.

Women have always been champions of the poor, of children, the old and helpless because somehow they have known that a great part of their happiness results from giving. And that in the last analysis it is our families and friends who hold the keys to our happiness. Ask any older person what brought him the greatest satisfaction and the answer is rarely career oriented. Usually it's his family, the children and grandchildren, and his close friends—not any success of itself but rather who shared it. A job you enjoy may be marvelously rewarding, but your triumphs can seem hollow if there's no one to share them with. A pat on the back from your boss is always nice but it can't hold a candle to a hug from someone who loves you. My conviction that priests should be allowed to marry has little to do with celibacy and a lot to do with loneliness.

To reach the top in your profession is a terrific kick. To have enough money is even better. But real success is not either one or both of those things. Jack's father spent his life working on the docks and has never lived a day without worrying about having enough money. His wife of fifty years loves him and twenty-two grandchildren know he's the best bicycle repairman, baseball coach and fishhook baiter in the world. And if you compare his life to Howard Hughes', it's very clear who achieved real success.

When women got swept up in the do-your-own-thing wave of the sixties and seventies, they seemed to lose all perspective. Often a husband, children and friends were cast aside by a woman wanting to be unencumbered by them as she entered the rat race of the business world. Many women began pushing for equality at any price—for satisfaction of self, for a total rejection of all things feminine by those who identify themselves as "feminists." Feminists used to be people who believed in the equality of women to men, but recently we've seen that word used to describe women who want superiority to men, who would form women's banks and women's insurance companies and are no more than female chauvinist sows whose motto is "nail the male."

These radical feminists antagonized many other women, and for the first time in the history of our country women are turning against women. Men always fought and squabbled, but women had more sense until the insanity of the 1970s. Today, women find themselves divided by semantics and specious arguments. And it need not happen. We have the chance for fuller, richer lives than our mothers and grandmothers ever dreamed of—equal education and job opportunities and unlimited horizons. But we should also be able to cling to the best of our values and not throw the baby out with the bath water. Women today should support each other, accepting and respecting each other's feelings. That would be true liberation.

Ms. Friedan made a point in her book that many housewife-mothers are openly resentful of working mothers, and it is often true. Not only were working mothers once an anomaly, but the home mothers often felt put upon by them and there were abuses. I had one friend who moved from a house she loved because she couldn't handle being held responsible for the children next door, whose working mother was never around when they needed her. Home mothers also felt justifiable resentment at being expected to serve as class mothers and field-trip chaperones, doing volunteer work with dizzying frequency because working mothers weren't available. But attitudes have changed. Not only is the working mother more accepted but the nonworking mother knows it is probably just a matter of time until she will be going off to a job and will be grateful for the support of her housewife neighbors.

As I said before, it is no longer a question of whether a woman will go out to work, but when. For almost every woman today, whatever her status or education, will eventually enter the work force. What is most telling is that our language has so few words to describe female workers and those we have are mostly for lower-echelon jobs like waitress and maid. About the only prestigious job with a female handle is "queen." Where important professions like doctor and judge are assumed to be male unless prefixed by "woman," the only jobs that have to be prefixed by "male" are nurse and secretary.

Whether or not there's a word for them, women

today are taking their places in the arts, sciences, business and government. They are being accepted as equals in most of the formerly all-male institutions, the Vatican and the U.S. Senate notwithstanding. (If a female aviator is an aviatrix, might a female senator be a senatrix?) We're training female astronauts, we have female governors. We even have female terrorists trying to prove that the world is no longer run by the hand that rocks the cradle but by the hand that cradles the rocket.

While women have the ability and the right to enter any profession or follow any career, it is blatantly unfair to tell them they must first relinquish their roles as mothers. No man is forced to choose between a family and a career. A man working in a small town may be expected to bolt out the door every time the fire whistle blows, but his boss is often reluctant to let a female employee leave to fetch a sick child from school. Men are routinely released from their jobs to fulfill commitments in the army reserve, but women's obligations are not so decently regarded.

Attitudes toward working housewives must be more realistic and understanding. Women who've postponed their careers for four to six years to give their children, America's hope of the future, a good start in life, deserve the same consideration given to returning war veterans. They too risked life and sanity in the interest of what they felt was the greater good. They too put the welfare of others before their own needs and aspirations. The degree of their hardships might vary, just as some veterans fought in trenches and others peeled potatoes at Fort Dix, but their intent was equal and so should be their reward. It is the final injustice to women to give them equality in the job market but then force them to choose between that job and raising their children.

Most working mothers are overburdened; they have two full-time jobs. What many need are meaningful part-time jobs for a few critical years, but the only ones generally available pay very poorly. Employers know there is an endless supply of housewives needing part-time work and so it is offered at very low wages with no fringe benefits. In all justice, if affirmative action is implemented to assure opportunities for minorities and the handicapped, why can't better provisions be made for the needs of working mothers, particularly those with advanced skills? Civil service jobs should be rewritten to be shared by two women and union regulations should be adjusted. Whatever paper work is necessitated by more complex arrangements would be more than compensated for in less-frequent employee turnover.

Our country is headed for a population crisis. Fewer children are being born and of those who are, an increasing majority is coming from underprivileged backgrounds, poorly nourished and educationally limited. Many are born to unwed teen-agers who may be incapable of giving a child the emotional support he needs. Our Social Security system will need a new base as great numbers of us reach retirement age while fewer able-bodied workers enter the labor force. Perhaps when this becomes a critical issue, motherhood for the middle class will be given new status and society will do more to accommodate the needs of the working mother. There might also be greater sensitivity toward the needs of our neglected poor children, the ones now too often discarded or disregarded, doomed from birth to lives of frustration, unemployment and welfare.

Working mothers are hardly a new phenomenon. Women have always worked, but married women rarely worked in other than family businesses. Until the Industrial Revolution, most men worked on farms or in shops with their wives at their sides. A professional man might leave his wife behind at home, but she would have a full-time job managing the household help when do-it-yourself was the only way and each home produced its own soap, yard goods and preserves.

If married women worked fifty years ago it was most likely that they were helping a husband get his business started. But my grandmother never knew, personally, a married woman with a career. Even unmarried women then rarely ever had more than a "position." In our family they were "in service" or "went to business."

The only woman in her family who had anything approaching a career was her sister Molly. Aunt Molly worked in the same factory as Grandma, but Grandma left to marry and Molly worked her way up to designing blouses. When she'd saved enough money, she and another Irish lady opened a small dress shop in Brooklyn, the likes of which will never be seen again.

They had a small front window where one dress was displayed and everything else was behind heavy wooden sliding doors which ringed the shop. No browsing through racks; they carefully brought out dresses one at a time and while the customer tried them on the ladies made tea. Each outfit was thoroughly discussed and Molly was ruthlessly honest, often telling a startled customer that they'd lower the hem to hide her awful legs. Or that no one with such a sallow complexion should even consider wearing yellow.

Aunt Molly was the kind of maiden aunt that hardly exists anymore. She had "neither chick nor child" but was loved by three generations of children. She was strong and determined, as any woman who succeeded in business in those days had to be. She drove a hard bargain with the Seventh Avenue manufacturers, who quickly learned that her ladylike manner was not a sign of weakness and that once she'd made up her mind, arguments were futile.

She was generous to a fault and every Christmas each household received, among other gifts, a subscription to the *Messenger of the Sacred Heart,* a monthly Catholic magazine. Once when her favorite nephew was very ill, Aunt Molly prayed to the Sacred Heart and told Him that if anything happened to Joseph, she intended to cancel all her subscriptions to His magazine. Joseph recovered promptly. Like all the men she did business with, the Sacred Heart knew better than to tangle with Aunt Molly.

CHAPTER

18

MINE WAS A FAMILY OF TALKERS. MAMA TOLD US each to please try to marry listeners. (They're very rare though.) One night at dinner my father shouted, "Stop. There are eleven people at this table and six are talking. Either pick up a listener or shut up." I mention this because one of the results of always fighting to get a word in edgewise was that we learned a kind of verbal shorthand, catch phrases mostly based on tag lines to old family stories.

We all knew what kind of a wedding it had been when told, "The bridesmaids looked like a bagful." An exercise in enlightened self-interest was described as "Another take a bite of your eclair." The line that comes to me now, in relation to children and how fast they grow up, came from a story my grandmother used to tell about a neighbor of hers in Brooklyn. The neighbor, Bridie, called Grandma one morning and said, "The party you had last night, was my Timmo there?" "Yes," said Grandma. "And was he drinking much?" "Yes," said Grandma. "And did he get to brawlin' and carryin' on?" "Well, he had himself a grand time," said Grandma. "Glory be to God, I was

afraid of that. Just tell me one last thing," said Bridie.
"Was I there?"

So it is with me and most mothers. One minute you
have a little baby and before you know it you're standing beside him at his high school graduation and you
can't figure where the time went. You know he had
a childhood; you have pictures to prove it. But you
find yourself asking, "Was I there?"

The one thing most difficult to explain to young
people is how quickly time passes. The young are so
impatient, so anxious to get on with the next thing.
I remember telling Mama how I couldn't wait until
the baby could walk or feed himself, and she'd say,
"Don't go wishing your life away." To a young mother,
the thought of giving up her job for four or five years
may seem an eternity. She can't know how fast the
time will whiz by.

Feeling such regret that those days with my children
went by so quickly, I can't imagine how cheated I'd feel
if I hadn't shared most of them. Many mothers cannot
be there because they must work. Most need the money
and some truly need to express or fulfill themselves.
But many working mothers are hardly coming out
ahead financially and are often working at dull and
boring jobs that demand time and energy, leaving
little of either for their children. Regrettably, I've
never personally known a child who talked to you
when you had set aside time to listen or had a crisis
in his life at your convenience.

Children, even adolescents, are so spirited and en-
ergetic that dealing with them takes strength and
stamina. And a parent must be involved with a child's

life. Children are like bank accounts—it's hard to withdraw without losing interest. And there are few things sadder than a youngster whose parents have lost interest, whose parents are uninvolved.

Children are fragile creatures with hearts easily broken, egos and self-confidence easily bruised. Yet sensitive people, who wouldn't leave their dog in a kennel every day or take their houseplants into a shocking environment, will drop their baby at a center whose greatest attribute is that it's convenient. There are some fine day-care facilities run by church groups or charitably motivated organizations like the YWCA, but now we are hearing about day care for profit— chains of centers scattered across the country to provide care for infants and toddlers. Horrible things occurred when care of the elderly became profitable; how much more vulnerable are little children, how much longer they will carry their scars.

Radical feminists would have us believe that twenty-four-hour day care is the answer to most of our problems, but it could cause more problems than it solves. In the first place, why would couples plan to have a child if they intended to have it raised by the government? Can you imagine the screams of civil libertarians if the state proclaimed that most of the women who bear children must turn them over to the state to be raised? The parents would be allowed to take their children home to sleep and for weekend visits, but their education and training would be in the hands of government employees. We cringed at George Orwell's idea of Big Brother, but are demanding Big Momma and Big Poppa.

Why would anyone who wasn't interested in raising a child plan to have one? Dogs make better pets and breeding chinchillas is a more profitable hobby. Children make rotten pets; they're messy, expensive to maintain and have been known to bite the hand that feeds them. And raising them is not a proper hobby. It isn't even a part-time job. It's very rewarding but requires great commitment, and commitment is not any more stylish than moderation or discretion, whether it be to children, spouses or elderly parents.

We live in an age of disposables, but children are not disposable, reusable or biodegradable. You can't throw them away if they turn out wrong. Having little patience, we treasure instant soup, instant gratification and instant replay. But there is no such thing as an instant adult. Too many ingredients are involved and too much attentive care required. The wrong ingredients and indifferent care can produce an adult, but not a very satisfactory one.

Part of the problem is that raising children is not very prestigious work today. Raising cattle or minks or orchids can reap rewards and approval, but children are our most undervalued natural resource. We have oil depletion allowances to protect energy sources, and well-meaning citizens chain themselves to trees to protect the environment. Rare animals are fiercely guarded and even ordinary animals are better protected than our children. A person who mistreats a pet is more likely to be reported to the authorities than one who cruelly abuses a child.

Priorities are all turned around by local agencies that spend more for faster highways than for youth programs and by a government that, as a matter of policy, pays more money to the people who handle our garbage pails than to the people who care for our elderly and handicapped, and now, our children.

Many experts on early-childhood development have reported on the effects of day care on small children, although it is difficult to judge the soundness of each theory. But a mother seems uniquely equipped to be the most important person in her child's world. She is, for instance, provided with the best possible food for him in her breast milk. I found nursing my babies a great joy and remember the first time my oldest child took notice of me breast-feeding his baby sister. He asked the obvious questions and I thought I handled it very well indeed, explaining how every baby needs special milk and nature provides its mother with just the right formula, and that when our baby came I was given this milk in my breast. As I was smugly congratulating myself for being so quick-witted, he asked, "But who punched the holes in the tips?"

Mothers seem blessed by nature with instincts for knowing by the sound of a child's cry whether he has gas or a disgusting diaper. She can look at his eyes and tell he is coming down with a fever. These qualities are not standard equipment in the average sitter, and it's hard to believe that it's best for a little baby to be handed over to a stranger or a series of strangers. As a naturalist friend of mine put it, monkeys know better than that.

Many women who wrote about their regrets at not staying home with their babies told stories of heartache when their small child fell or cut himself and ran past their outstretched arms to the baby-sitter for comfort. These mothers felt they'd missed too much—and that's the point. Whether or not day care is best for the baby may be debatable, but it's hard to believe it's best for most mothers. Particularly today's mothers who are having only one or two children, so we're talking about an investment of five or six years. She'd take that much time to get a graduate degree, why not take it for something even more important in terms of her overall life? Why miss an experience that can never be repeated, an opportunity that can never be recaptured?

At no time in life do the changes come faster than in the first few years. The little blob who first looks like Winston Churchill without the cigar soon turns into a person with character and personality and a frown like his father and a disposition like your mother-in-law. You watch to see his first step, then long to see him slow down for a minute. You thrill to hear his first words and soon wonder if he'll ever stop asking questions. And the thing is, he needs you like he'll never again need you or anyone else, and filling that need gives no small satisfaction. When he gets to college and relies on you only to send some "bread," you'll remember fondly the days when all he needed to be happy was your lap and a box of animal crackers.

I don't suggest it's easy taking care of babies and toddlers. It is exhausting and frustrating most of the time, but there are brief shining moments scattered among the long days that manage to pull things into perspective. I had four babies in four years and it was no picnic. During that time, Jack was working all day, going to law school at night and weekends. When he finally finished school and passed the bar, the first job he had paid seventy dollars a week, so he worked weekends as a dishwasher at a restaurant (young lawyers can't very well work as waiters or check-out clerks lest they be observed by a potential client whose faith in them would certainly crumble). Summers were better because he pushed a Good Humor ice-cream wagon around a distant town and made real money. Although as an ex-Marine officer and new member of the bar, it was a little humiliating to be constantly asked, "Hey, kid, what's the flavor of the week?"

Sounds like a nightmare, doesn't it? Well, it was one of the best times of our lives. Financially, we would have been better off if I'd worked after the fourth baby came, but we both felt it wouldn't have been better for the children. My sanity was put to test after test (failing several), but next door were my mother, helping by baby-sitting, and my grandmother, helping by reminding me that these were the best years of my life. Some days that was not what I wanted to hear (or believe) and if she hadn't been in a wheelchair I'd have been tempted to whack her with my diaper bag. But seeing that frail old lady and remembering the dynamo she once was, running around her own house, clucking over her chicks, doing for them and their father, touching each of them every day, I had to know in my heart she was right. Certainly I treasured my children more, remembering the terrible pain in my grandmother's eyes that summer afternoon in 1944 when the telegram came saying, "We regret to inform you of the death of your son, Corporal Frank O'Donohue. . . ."

Often when I'd complain to Grandma about how hard I was finding motherhood, she would listen sympathetically and softly tell me that one day I'd give everything I owned just to relive that hard time. So, many a night spent pacing around with a teething baby I'd remember her words and realize someday I'd pay any price to bring back that weary moment. Many a cold afternoon as I stood on a windy corner waiting for the school bus, I'd think how someday I'd give anything to have a little boy jump off that bus and run into my arms.

When we first moved to our house the children's bathroom was filled with boats and rubber ducks and Mister Bubble. Then suddenly they were all gone— replaced by blow dryers and Clearasil. The boys' bedroom had been a sea of toy trucks and cars and small soldiers and the whole Apache nation in miniature, which you always seemed to step on barefoot. No rampaging warrior ever inflicted more pain. Then before I knew what was happening, the room became plastered with posters and banners and STOP signs, and a stereo blared incessantly. And now it's deadly quiet in there except for summers and college semester breaks. The little boys whom you washed and dressed for years are young men who say "Aw, Ma, lemme alone" when you try to straighten a shirt collar. The little boys who once had to tell you everything, twice, now answer all your questions with "Don't worry about it, Ma." So you worry.

With daughters it's worse, for they grow independent more quickly. The doll house you finally got completely furnished was relegated to the attic the same year, replaced by a mirrored dressing table awash with cosmetics and rollers. The little girl who loved dressing up in your clothes now looks on your wardrobe with undisguised pity. The little girl whose hair you braided every morning now doesn't want you to touch it because it's taken hours to get that wisp to fall just over her left eye.

And suddenly, for every mother, there comes a day when the house is strangely quiet and there are no school books on the kitchen table and no hockey sticks in the umbrella stand and no one yells, "Hey, Ma, I'm home!" or "What's for dinner?" And no matter how full your life, how successful your career (even if you've just published a book), you look into the mirror and see a middle-aged woman staring back at you, both of you wondering, "Where are the children?" Both of you wondering, "Was I there?"